THE JOYFUL CHILD

Vinnie —
A gift from
your friends.
Best
[illegible]
Kentville
Oct '11

wayzgoose

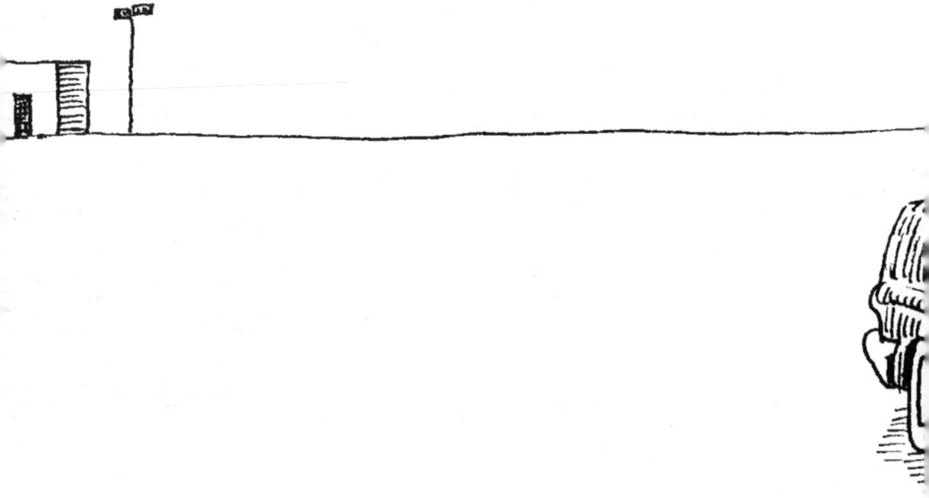

GASPEREAU PRESS ✦ PRINTERS & PUBLISHERS ✦ 2011

The Joyful Child

NORMAN RAVVIN

With illustrations by Melanie Boyle

THE OLD CAR GUYS

It was the three of us, me, Stitchman and Paul, a year ago almost to the day. It was the end of August. The first leaves were down. And it was one of the last times we maintained our custom of meeting up on a weekend morning. Our jalopies were parked nose to end on the narrow street. Stitchman's cucumber green Thunderbird. Paul's toaster car, as we liked to call it. My rusted black Sedan de Ville, just barely getting by on its old rubber. We were known in the neighbourhood as the old car guys. Some seemed amused, and others definitely disapproved, judging by the smiles of camaraderie and sneers of derision that greeted me, depending on who was behind the counter at the grocery, the library, or the gas station down Bloor. We'd met each other at Stitchman's garage, and this was the glue holding us together. He was our avenue to cheap auto parts and free labour. He and I were exquisite loners, familyless men in a world that seemed full of parenting. After my thirtieth birthday I'd more or less accepted that I was one of the city's true bachelors. I had left home as a teenager, and had more or less forgotten what family life felt like. Paul, on the other hand, was newly swamped by fatherhood. His young son Nick had come to live with him, after the prospect of an offer in the United States led Nick's mother to agree that the boy should stay put rather than follow her.

Stitchman and I cajoled Paul into bringing his Nash out of the oily garage behind his house. That's how we found ourselves in the back alley, watching Paul turn his key in the ignition, looking as if he were about to discover electricity.

"Dead," he said, confirming the obvious.

"Well, when did you drive it last?" Stitchman asked.

Paul couldn't say. We brought my car around—filled the whole alleyway with it—and hooked his up for a boost.

"Let it run," Stitchman said. He lit a cigarette and did something that always amazed me: he leaned in under Paul's hood, ashes bright and smoking in one hand, to check on the carburetor he'd repaired a few months back.

Paul waved a sheet of note paper, a couple of inches by four, that Nick had scribbled on.

"What do you think it is? Huh? Come on guys, forget the cars. Guess."

From under the hood Stitchman mumbled something.

"Hey," Paul said. "Come out of there. I want you to see this."

I took the scrap of paper. On it in black ball point ink

was a thicket of child's scribblings, a base of overlapping circles crisscrossed by up and down lines. Stitchman came out from under the hood and took it from me.

"Hey, come on." Paul grabbed the paper. "I'm saving that. I don't want grease prints on it."

Stitchman backed up a step and slammed the hood of the car a good deal harder than was necessary. "You're going to have to tell us," he said, wiping his hands on his jeans, "what the child genius did this time?"

"All right." Paul held the paper so the scribbles faced out at us. "He said it's a picture of the world's biggest fart."

"He said it like that?" Stitchman liked to bug Paul about his parental devotion.

"Yah. What do you mean?"

"Like an adult, in good grammar?"

"Okay, okay." Paul slipped the note paper into his wallet and sat on the trunk of the Nash.

This was the last time the three of us got together. Who could have guessed how, for Paul and Nick, everything would change in the coming year?

We talked about our storage plans for our jalopies. I was the odd man out. I'd drive the Cadillac across the lake if that turned out to be the best way to Buffalo. It was a thing, just a thing I'd stumbled upon when a friend was unloading possessions cheap. Two hundred dollars and a day's work dislodging the junk that had accumulated in the back seat and the trunk. But for my two friends life was not so simple. Stitchman had given his practical car—a rust-smeared Toyota—to his ex after she'd bolted their disastrous year together. This meant, and he said this as if it represented some sort of medieval torture worse than death, that he would either have to ride the transit all winter or run the Thunderbird, even after the city began throwing road salt. Road salt. The nemesis of old car guys and gals alike. Sometimes we loitered over a coffee and daydreamed about Arizona. Santa Monica. Red Rock Valley, Nevada. Mythic places where the worst thing the climate could do to a car was heat up the chrome door handles so they burned you if you forgot to grab them with something other than bare skin.

I saw him next on the corner of Bloor and Bathurst, clutching a paper cup full of cold coffee. I asked if he'd seen Paul and he shrugged.

"They were in the shop. We put the kid in the car and ran it up on the hoist. I think he thought we were sending him to the moon."

"The kid's grown," Stitchman said, as though this surprised him, as if he expected Nick to stay the same forever—bare-limbed, careless and perfectly inquisitive. These things happen: children grow, their parents age. But I saw Paul and Nick often enough to miss the changes' finer points. I noticed the little things, which Paul had a habit of jotting down so he would be able to check when Nick stopped saying geen in favour of green, mowf in favour of mouth. When he insisted on going to the bathroom all by myself.

"Paul's changed, too. Even from across the street you

could tell. Something in the face. I don't know how to describe it."

He drank from his cup and breathed. "Smell."

"Smell what?"

"Smell," he answered, his face bright.

I caught the slightest hint of lake, or woods or something else renewed that blew our way up Bathurst.

KIND OF BLUE

They went down on the train. They were improvising. The city was brutally cold, snow-white and strange, but still, it was something different from what they knew back in Toronto. In the parks, nobody was out. It was just the snow and the wrought iron against the diamond blue sky. Paul and Mary came up with a routine. They'd walk a few blocks, admire the architecture and the people in their romantic overcoats, then they would look, almost in panic from the cold, for another café au lait, the soft warm white bowl by the windows that looked out onto St. Laurent or Ste. Catherine or Mount Royal. Streets they knew only from poetry books they'd read. To think that they were ever young enough to get their information from poems.

The apartment was borrowed from a couple who were splitting up. He was in Japan with someone new, and she, back home with her parents in British Columbia. The apartment block seemed barely held together behind its impressive stone facade and frilly green mansard roof.

They trudged up three winding flights of wooden stairs,

and felt, immediately, as though they'd stumbled onto a movie set. The soundtrack awaited them in the kitchen, in a tape machine that was outdated, pawnshop bought. It sat on a peeling paint table by the window, which was sealed with plastic against the cold. Paul pressed play and Miles Davis came out. Rivery blue meditations and jazz nocturnes. Cool 1959 piano, electric, glowing. The trumpet voicing a language they couldn't speak, but a language all the same, brooding and unpredictable. It was perfect music to go with the pathos of the old building, the harshness of the cold blue day.

¶ When Paul told me all this, it was difficult to believe it had happened more than a decade before. In another life entirely. Back when he was still with Mary, the only woman he'd ever imagined living with. She had changed him, had pulled him from his old life in Vancouver, where he'd spent his teenage years and early twenties fancying himself to be some kind of throwback to the Beats, thriving on conversation, good weather, bad coffee and cheap draft. The latter he drank in Gastown bars he'd discovered as a teenager, never moving on to something more with-it. It felt good to be inside those places, in the beer-smelling dark, watching the tourists walk by outside. He'd earned a meager living writing rock reviews for the Georgia Straight, and he'd lived in a succession of tumbledown houses along the defunct, morning glory-strewn rail line at the southerly edge of Kitsilano.

Mary had cleaned up his act in no time. It was her idea

to move to Toronto. What did he know? He'd never been east of the Crowsnest Pass. So they went. They set up on Markham Street, in one of the tall gingerbread houses, most of which were filled with large Azorean families—the teenagers saving their money by living with their parents, and the pampered butterball kids being fattened up for more love and feeding. The old-timers sat, impassive, on their front porches, behind dark glasses, antique walking sticks between their knees. At first Paul tried waving. What the hell, he thought, they think I'm a reprobate, some sort of white trash intruder, but we're neighbours all the same. When the waves failed, he tried the serious and, he thought, manly nod of recognition. He tried every hand signal he could think of, but the old-timers stared him down like he was a fence post. They won: they had nerves of steel in the battle over whether you waved or did not wave at strangers on Markham Street.

In Toronto it seemed to Paul that Mary developed a new personality. She became a woman so dedicated to her career that anything that could be seen to impede it, from friendships to the possibility of having a family, was deemed a waste of time. They were young enough when they first arrived that the question of children never came up. Children were something old people thought about.

With her inheritance Mary bought them a house in Cabbagetown, across from the Riverdale Farm and the woods where the monarch butterflies congregate in the summer. All of a sudden the monarchs would pile in, with Mexico in their wings, and lay up against each other in the branches. They seemed to sleep, swaying on a humid afternoon, so thick and bristling a crush of them that they gave off their own scent, a skunky, cinnamon cloud that wafted across the street and through Paul's study window.

❨With time, Paul and Mary found they were becoming strangers to one another. They were too busy with day-to-day routines to have a proper conversation, and months went by in a faceless rush. With each new coming of spring they made an effort to pull things together, to make it all work the way it had in the years when they had nothing, no plans, just a sense of everything being possible. The house provided a certain stability. Together they protected the daffodils and tulips from predatory squirrels, dropping garlic cloves and mothballs to give the sprouts a chance. They brought the car out on the pavement and washed it clean of the winter's salt and crusted mud. And every now and then they walked in the wooded park behind the zoo and tried to tell each other how they felt, what they were thinking. Who it was, exactly, they had each become.

But as summer came on, the familiar feelings of defeat and entrapment would press down on them like thought bubbles in a comic book. What were they doing? Was this adult life as it was meant to be? Mary dug in deeper and deeper at work, so there was almost nothing left when she got home in the evening. She worked at a law firm that specialized in immigrants and refugee claims. Although she didn't have the degree that would have given her the credentials her position demanded, she read like a demon, and the lawyers at the clinic gave her the time she needed to get the hang of research and writing briefs. By the time she'd been at it a year she might as well have had the law degree. She was a tiger. Most of the clients she supported got into the country. She threw herself into her work in a way that made Paul uncomfortable. They had less and less time for the simplest things, like having dinner together or sharing the Sunday Times. They went from seeing a movie once a week to once a month. Often Paul made the trek himself to the theatres on Yonge Street. As he trudged over, the windows of the big brick Victorian houses seemed to wink at him, as if to make fun of his lonesomeness. And by the time he made it to the theatre he felt like a single guy again, the young man he'd been when Mary and he had first met in a Vancouver coffee house, and no one—no one—had any call on how he spent his days. He sat alone in an aisle seat, halfway down the theatre, and laughed out loud if the film was half funny, just to hear himself.

While Mary's commitment to her work deepened, her energy ever fiercer, Paul found himself drifting. He gave up on the music reviews he'd written for the Toronto papers. The endless concert-going had left him with an intermittent buzz in his head, like the one the refrigerator made at night. His main business became that of a careful house-manager—a house husband, in the style of the day, but without the usual child-raising responsibilities. He cleaned the stove, vacuumed, shopped, arranged visits from roofers, chimney sweeps and firewood suppliers. Still, when all of this was done, he had too much time on his hands. So he went back to an adolescent love of his—the guitar. He found a teacher who was willing to come to the house and endured the man's weekly passive-aggressive response to Paul's efforts. Practising was not his forte. So, whether it was "Greensleeves" or the intricacies of a twelve-bar blues, he performed the weekly project with a distinct feeling of failure. When the teacher had left, taking his sparkling Gibson guitar and his handful of long pointed fingernails, buttressed by some kind of product for horse hoofs he bought at a veterinary supply store, Paul reverted to the songs that came easily. Three chord chestnuts from Neil Young songbooks, and the choruses from his generation's anthems, like Lou Reed's "Sweet Jane," which seemed to offer a philosophy for living in the beauty of their simplicity. Guitar playing distracted him from the big questions that hovered unendingly. What were they doing? Where was it all heading? Outside, the butterflies hung, jostling one another, smelling of burnt gingerbread.

¶So it goes without saying that Paul was surprised when Mary suggested they have a child. Straight out of the blue, over dinner.

"Let's try," she said, looking serious and a little sad.

Paul didn't know what to say. He had no good reason to say no. Even if they got pregnant that evening he'd have another nine months of house-husbandry and his own mediocre efforts to become the next Bob Dylan. So, yes. He said yes. They left the dishes on the table and went upstairs. The butterflies seemed to watch through the bedroom window as they undressed. Without kissing they lay down together and made love. Paul thought that he should remember how it felt, because the child might be there from this evening on. The weird outcome of this was that making love felt to him like thinking.

¶Nick was born in a green-painted hospital room with a view of a grey cathedral where the old-timers from Portuguese islands still carried on the old rituals. The remarkable things about his birth were these: the amniotic sac that preceded him refused to break, a tough globe of birth fluid and whatever else protruding from his mother, so Paul was given the opportunity to break it, which he did, whereupon he passed out, collapsing in free fall, smashing his jaw on the linoleum floor. This ensured that mother and son were released from hospital sooner than the new father. And though TV pundits say that when a baby is born there is a reflexive cry with the first breaths, Nick did not follow this pattern. Paul's first memory of Nick is of him lying in his mother's arms, straight-faced, busily but quietly drawing breath through puckered lips. From these first breaths forward, it can be said that who Nick would become was apparent. His personality, his humour, his inclinations and rhythms all derive from those first breaths. A few minutes old and he was already busy just being himself. His parents called him Nick—not short for Nicholas, or after Nick Adams, Nick Drake and all the rest of the likely models—because it was short and to the point.

The child arrived in spring. They had no time for the usual spring cleaning, and the yard lay grey and crusted with leaves and the leavings of melted snow. Mary took a look at the earnings from her inheritance, at the bank accounts and the cost of maintaining the house. They could easily get by without her salary. The day she quit they rolled Nick in his stroller to Cherry Beach and sat looking out at the water, which looked boundless, like their own newfound ability as Nick grew, to attend to his needs, night and day.

The lack of sleep was difficult, but not distressingly so, since neither of them had anywhere they had to be on the morning after a sleepless night. From time to time, when Nick took one of his rare naps, Paul would steal into his study to try to concentrate on a blues lick his teacher had shown him much too quickly to get the full idea, so the best he could do was work on a round of country and western chords. Big fat clangers that only sound good after six beer. His head was full of diapers and burps and feedings and the child's expressions—wide eyes gazing, the little mind taking in its first sense of what the world was about. When his fingertips ached from the metal strings he sat at his desk and stared through the window at the trees. He listened to himself breathe in the unlikely quiet. Sometimes he sat long enough that the moon appeared to darken and slip downward in the sky. Stars glittered. Cars whispered by on the pavement.

❨Although Paul and Mary loved the child fiercely, his arrival did not resolve their differences. In fact, their love for the child seemed to replace any love they might have shared with each other. They continued to fight, quietly, out of Nick's earshot, about nearly everything. There was even something new—how to deal with the child when he wouldn't sleep or eat. Paul's usual response was not to worry. Mary, on the other hand, broke out the child-rearing books and got on the phone to her friends. When they were both exhausted by Nick's exuberant sleeplessness, and by their own feelings of entrapment at the thought of more and more of the same pointless arguing, Paul began to consider moving out. But he hesitated, when a friend who practised family law told him that if he were the one to go it would hurt him in a custody battle. This sort of behaviour, Paul's friend said, reminds a judge of those guys on sinking ships who elbow women and children out of the way to get onto the last lifeboat. In the end it didn't matter. The possibility of being away from Nick hurt him inside so badly that he abandoned the idea of leaving as his answer to what was wrong.

Then two things happened out of the blue, a bit like Mary's suggestion that led to Nick's birth. The first of these was the resurfacing of Paul's father, not in body, but in deed. A package came, via registered mail, from a law firm in Long Island. The stuff inside was slapped with so many stamps and signatures you could have mistaken it for the man's will. Bill Hunt had in fact died, and upon reading his will, his second family—people he'd made his life with for decades, whom Paul had never heard of—discovered that he had left one of his most valuable assets to a son in Canada. Paul's father had apparently become a very rich man in the years after he abandoned his son and wife in their suburban New York bungalow. The piece of his fortune that he'd set aside for his abandoned son turned out to be a collection of vintage cars. It was housed in a cold storage garage in New Jersey, and numbered more than twenty vehicles. These included old American muscle cars with spectacularly shiny chromed engines; a Jaguar coupe; a big old Bentley; and oddities like a pair of two-tone Metropolitan Nashes, one with blue accents, the other pink. The lawyer's letter included a photo package, professionally arranged in plastic envelopes, highlighting the best specimens in the collection.

The lawyer wanted to know what to do. Should he sell the lot at auction? Did Paul want to visit the cars himself? Did he want one shipped up to Toronto, just for fun? When Paul suggested to Mary that he go down and look at his treasure before he decided what to do with it, she became more enraged than he'd ever seen her.

"Not on your life," she shouted. "Not on your goddamn life." At this point in their relationship, Mary took most ideas he had for himself as an excuse to shirk his duties at home. He felt a twinge as he dialed the lawyer at a Jersey number. They chatted and the man sang the cars' praises. "They're beauties," he enthused. "Jewels on wheels. If you don't get them out of here, some mafia guy's gonna steal 'em out from under your nose. Or your relatives down here—you know, they've got resources."

Paul okayed the sale of the lot. What, he wondered, were they evaluated at?

The lawyer suggested the full shot, after taxes, could net almost a million dollars U.S. "These things are big here now, after 9/11. Everyone's after a piece of the past. They all wanna buy their way back to a time before it all got unclear."

"I'll keep one," Paul said, almost without thinking. "Send me one of those Nashes. The two-tone blue on white."

Did Paul want the car right away? The lawyer wondered.

"Yes," he heard himself saying. "Send it as soon as you can."

When the car arrived, chained to the floor of a freight car at the port of Toronto, Paul went down without telling Mary what was up. He watched as the car was unloaded on the siding. Up against the graffiti-scarred boxcar, it looked like a little blue and white jewel. He sat inside. Ran his hand over the upholstery and over the chromed space-age laminate on the dash. The odometer read 1001 and the motor was so well tuned it barely made a sound when he started it up. Running, it reminded him of an electric can opener that sat on the kitchen counter through his childhood. He drove the car around for an hour or so—over to the Beaches, through the downtown, along College and down to Harbourfront—before he pointed it at their house. He pulled up on the driveway and honked.

When Mary saw him her lips got visibly thinner and tighter. Whiter even. As if she were biting them.

The Nash became one more topic in their long list of disagreements. Was he going to pay for a second car? This was a clear shot at the fact that Mary paid the bills, a reminder that he had been a kind of freeloader in his own house.

The fact that the car had belonged to his father didn't interest her at all. Why be sentimental about the asshole who'd abandoned him?

So Paul was careful to park the Nash across the street. Sometimes he went out to it, opened the passenger door, and sat with his feet on the pavement as he breathed in the butterfly-smell wafting out of the trees. It was then—just then—that he felt happy.

❨What came out of the blue next was worse, worse than anything, and it had its own unlikely repercussions.

On an afternoon when Paul was out of the house, Mary very nearly burned the place to the ground. Making his way home, as he neared their block, Paul smelled wood smoke and heard the chatter of police radios. Two fire trucks idled in the street, their big emergency lights turning and spotlighting the neighbours' houses in red and gold. Nick and Mary stood across the street from their home, wrapped in silver blankets under the cover of the pine trees where the butterflies congregated. Nick stared, mouth wide, at what was left of the house. The drama that surrounded him happened to include fire trucks, which were among his great loves. He looked like a character in one of his own books: half real, half cartoon; eyes so big they had to be fake.

The house was gutted. The brick facade stood, but the insides were charred black. The firemen were putting water on the last few hot spots. The cracked window of Paul's study emitted the smoke of burnt bedding and scorched carpet. He thought of his guitar, burning crisply, laquer bubbling off its face, until the strings popped free, and this was followed by a perverse moment when he realized he could cancel his lesson for the coming week.

As Paul rushed over, Nick began to cry, then Mary after him. They said they were okay. They'd escaped in good time. Mary tried to explain something about an oven mitt left on the stove top. Flames spitting up into the overhead fan so quietly that it took Nick, who whispered, Mama, to alert her to what was happening behind her back. Before she could do a thing, the old plywood cupboards were ablaze, flames pushing through the ceiling and out the back windows. Mary had grabbed Nick. The neighbours on one side—the ones who were always first to let them know they'd left their car on the wrong side of the street—had called 911. Then mother and son stood under the trees while the house burned.

The three of them watched the firefighters drag bits of

scorched furniture out onto the lawn to douse them. Then the men carefully packed up their gear and drove away. The whole scene looked fake. How could a family's home go up in flames while the neighbours went on with their day? The street was utterly quiet, except for the sound of tire treads on the wet pavement as cars slipped slowly by, rubberneckers in the passenger seats trying to get a look at the disaster. A few neighbours stood in their open front doors and stared. Paul imagined that he knew their thoughts: Thank goodness it was over there and not here. One offered to put them up for the night, and Mary said yes without asking Paul or Nick how they felt. So they slept on the living room floor in a house down the street from their own charred home.

The next morning they woke early, and without eating breakfast, or even stopping for a cup of coffee, walked down the block to see what was left of the house. Nick said it smelled like barbecued hot dogs. And he was right. At first they thought they might go inside and pull out anything that hadn't been completely burnt, but they stopped at the doorstep, astounded. The inside of the house was a big black and grey mass. Walls hung in midair, and the main floor ceiling was gone. When Nick looked into the darkened space that had been their home he began to cry, the kind of blubbering tears that he'd cried as a baby. Even the little red and yellow plastic car they had left on the front porch had been melted down to the size of a plate. The only artifacts of their lives, pre-fire, were the yard's great tall oaks, and the Nash in its spot across the street.

Heads down, they walked up the road to a diner they liked. Paul was certain everyone in the place was staring at them, as if they knew that this was the homeless family, the people who had burnt down their own house. Still, they sat and ordered and chatted about what needed to be done next, as if it were a normal morning. What came next was a wide open question. The list was enormous. Nick needed clothes. The insurance people had to be met with. Friends would have to be told. They needed a post office box and a new phone number. Mary was fixated on their need for a rental car. "I'm not," she said, with brutal seriousness, "driving Nick around in your dad's little old tin can."

To their amazement, their household insurers agreed to put them up in a hotel for the short term. And because the allowance for accommodations was so generous, they ended up in a suite downtown, overlooking the lake. Nick slept in the back bedroom, with the TV softly humming for company, a luxury he'd never imagined existed.

The hotel suited Nick perfectly: TV, swimming pool, restaurant meals, attentive staff who seemed to feel it was part of their job to let him describe his day at length, including the doings of a raft of imaginary friends who were apparently with him at the hotel—Bruce, a character based on a plumber who'd once come to the house; Topham Hatt, a tuxedoed, top-hatted character borrowed from the train set he collected; and Bubbie, that is, Nick's great-grandmother, a woman he had heard of but never met. The four of them, according to Nick's rambling narratives, spent their time riding elevators, resting in their rooms, putting on their bathing suits, and playing in the pool. Nick's one variation on the actual hotel amenities was that there was a morning pool and an afternoon pool. The bottom line was that he, Topham Hatt and Bruce spent most of their time getting ready, going to, and coming back from the pool. Sometimes Bubbie was waiting for them in their room, where they would all hold hands, talk, and take a well-deserved nap before the next pool adventure. Or, as Nick put it, aventure. For him the hotel was one supreme aventure.

For Mary and Paul it was madness. They spent their days trading off, one taking care of Nick while the other met with a parade of lawyers and insurance agents to try to get their life back. Their insurance company, still the good guys in the pack, had agreed to rebuild the house. This was astounding. By some stroke of luck, when Mary had bought the place, she had chosen a gold-plated policy without even meaning to. But the outcome of this largess was many more meetings. Because the house was across the street from the butterflies' resting woods, construction on their property was restricted by long, nearly incomprehensible bylaws. Architects, city zoning clerks, contractors, carpenters, even neighbours had to be included in discussions, to make sure the new house didn't overstep. With the insurance money they would be able to rebuild the house as a brighter, crisper, better-planned version of its old Victorian self. Goodbye plywood kitchen cupboards. Finish date was late summer. Possibly fall.

What would they do until then? Live like fugitives in the Westin Harbour Castle? Listening day after day to Nick's doings with the invisible Bruce and Topham Hatt? This looked about as grim as things could get.

One night, late, after finally convincing Nick that Bruce and Topham Hatt were asleep in their rooms, this being proof that he, too, should be asleep, Mary and Paul sat on the balcony overlooking the lake. It was one of those rare summer evenings in Ontario that everyone wishes would go on forever. The new leaves were in the trees. The lake was a crisp, balmy green beneath the moon. And the air smelled of water. You could almost believe the lake was the sea. That it rolled on forever, all the way to foreign lands.

Mary slumped in her chair, a glass of beer between bare legs. She looked exhausted. Haggard. Not so much sad as stunned. Blankly amazed at what had become of their life.

Without looking at Paul, Mary said, "Let's go to the sea."

Paul sat back, gazed out at the lake, and waited for more.

"The house won't be ready for months. I don't know if I want to go back to work at all. You're waiting for your inheritance to arrive in a registered letter from New Jersey. Let's get Nick out of this place. I saw an ad in the paper today. A rental on one of the islands out west. We can see if the insurance people will let us switch it for this. Why wouldn't they? It would cost them less. And we can tell them Nick wants to be nearer to his great-grandmother while everything works itself out. That he's undergoing some sort of trauma. We can get the doctor to write something." This couldn't have been further from the truth. Nick loved the hotel. He wanted to grow up there. He already had fashioned a new identity for himself, based on a character in one of his books: he was Nick, the lost boy, who lived in a hotel by the water.

Mary lifted the beer for a drink, then licked foam from her upper lip. "What do you think?"

Paul gazed out at the water. He wondered if the boy's imaginary companions would all come along west.

¶ They picked up their rental car on Georgia Street and drove through the Vancouver traffic to the ferry terminal. The car was a Toyota, with its butt comically raised on its back wheels, like a rabbit set to run. Nick was smitten. He embarked on a new project, to point out every car like it that passed them. It was this, Paul thought, that vanquished Bruce and Topham Hatt. New province, new fascination. Back home the family car was too smoke-damaged to drive. The insurance people had not yet decided what its value was, which seemed to be a bad sign. The two-tone Nash was in a cold storage garage in Mississauga, squeezed in with the prized vehicles of rich men under flourescent lights.

The vista from the roadway that approached the ferry terminal took their breath away. Nick stared, as if he could not comprehend the mix of ocean and festooned freighters, the landscape surrounding them like the palm of a giant spirit-hand offering the view. They drove in silence, like strangers on a bus. First Paul rolled down his window. Then Mary did the same. From the back, Nick began to whine. He wanted his window down too. So Mary reached around and rolled it down, and the hot ocean breeze blew through the car.

In the ferry lineup Nick decided he wanted to go home. The gulls, he announced, were bugging him. But once the wait was over, and they had motored on board, his view changed. An aventure was clearly beginning. Fishing boats floated alongside the ferry like little houses—worlds in themselves—bouncing in the blue blue water.

A fantasy land. Fairy tale houses afloat in the sea. Faraway, magic mountains.

"We can live here," Nick announced. "We can live on this ferry boat."

❨The ferry docked with a shiver. They drove out onto the Island Highway, at first just another Canadian ribbon of strip malls, gas stations, and fast food outlets, with its own unique grotesquerie: a flurry of lurid billboards advertising water slides and casinos. But this gave way to another green world. As they drove, Paul and Mary recognized in the expanses of forest and sky, in the difference of the landscape from what they knew back home, the possibility of the kind of rest they needed.

Still, even Nick noticed that something was not right.

"Talk!" he shouted from the back seat. "Talk!"

His parents drove on into the afternoon, barely saying a word to each other. They took turns at the wheel, each wearing Paul's sunglasses, because Mary's had been swallowed by the fire and she'd not yet found a replacement pair. Eventually, Nick fell asleep in the rented car seat, his breath quiet, insistent, like a cat's snore. The soft air coming in at the windows lulled Mary to sleep, too, so that Paul pushed onward, alone. The car moved toward the Island's western shore. The house they'd rented near Sooke was not available till the following morning, so they had planned to find something cheap nearby. One of them could get Nick to bed while the other went shopping to get stocked up for the coming weeks.

Not far outside Victoria, Paul saw a sign advertising a farmhouse for rent: "Nightly or Weekly Rates. Clean and Cozy." Paul stopped at a pay phone and got directions. He followed a road hidden from the highway by a tree nursery's stand of young pine until a house came into view. Paul pulled up and got out of the car, shutting the door quietly so as not to wake his wife and child. He stood and looked in at them through the dusty windshield, then gazed at the forest behind the property, breathed deep to smell it, and felt better, just from that one lungful. He found the owner of the property in his vegetable garden hoeing around the beans and radish. The man said "Howdy," shook Paul's hand, and gave him the key. He explained that the house was divided into two halves, part of which was his own family's home. "Usually," he said, "I'd bring my kid over to meet yours, but he's got a big test tomorrow. Makeup for one he failed in the spring, and he's nervous as hell. See you in the morning," he said over his shoulder as he went back to work.

While Mary and Nick slept on in the car, Paul got things ready inside. There was a mat on the floor that could be Nick's bed. He checked the pots and pulled out what they'd need to make dinner. Behind a wall he thought he could hear the man who'd said howdy talking to someone sternly, explaining something once and then again.

Much later, Mary and Paul were awakened by what sounded like a child's cry, followed by little feet stomping to a spot where they stopped, just behind the wall where the bed stood. They heard the child retch, moan, and call out first for his mommy and then for daddy. They listened as the boy mumbled something about not wanting the morning to come. Then things went quiet for a while. Outside, high in the trees, an owl called, a long slow cry. Then it was all repeated: child's feet, a lurching stop behind the wall, more moaning and the whirl of the flushing toilet. Nick slept through it all as if nothing were happening.

Paul and Mary sat up in bed and stared at the bare wood-paneled walls. This late night upset brought them back to themselves, after the day's travels—the rare light and hot dry roads. It brought them back to their love for Nick, in his innocence and open-heartedness. And to the awareness, in the dark, with the owl calling to them from the treetops, that they had no idea what came next.

GOODBYE, CHA-CHAROO

They took two tiny car ferries to get to Hornby Island. There, they sampled what was left of the old summer of love—it was as if they'd gone way, way back in time, only to discover a hidden world of hemp artists and tambourine shakers and sandalistas, who reminded Paul of the heyday of such types on West Fourth in Vancouver. In his memory, addled by nostalgia and too many cases of Pilsner Old Stock, the hippies lay loose on the ground back then, like a rich crop of pumpkin.

"Should we stay over?" Paul asked. To which Nick hollered, "Yes!" But Mary had an appointment in Victoria, with someone who had been trying to convince her to start work, part time, in a firm like the one where she'd worked in Toronto. The ferry schedule made it impossible for her to be there on time if they didn't head back by the end of the day. Nick cried, but only for a moment, at learning that there was something more important than Hornby Island loafing. "OK momma," he said quietly. "I understand."

It had been a blue blue day. They sailed home after dinner. The trees were backlit by the sunset and looked like paper cut-outs. Smoke from a mill stack billowed over the water in fat shifting belly-flops. The gulls flapped toward the ferry in neat lines, and a flock of hot-air balloons appeared in the sky above the calm water. The three of them pointed and shouted.

"Montgolfière!" Nick shouted again and again. He'd learned the French word in preschool, and had decided, after teaching it to his parents, that its frilly, fruity syllables were the best way to describe the hoosh of hot air, the bright flame-coloured canvas, and the dangling wicker baskets with their pinpoint-sized pilots waving down at them.

From above, at a distance, Nick, Paul and Mary must have looked like one more young, happy family. This would be, in a corny, feel-good film, their establishing shot: the threesome in their newly bought Gore-Tex jackets and hiking shoes, standing in for central casting versions of adventurers on the wild coast. Paul and Mary were lean and tanned. Her head reached just above his shoulders, his hair unruly in the wind. The boy was the colour of chestnut—his hair and his outsized eyes beneath girlish lashes. Nick alone gazed off the front of the boat with full-hearted enthusiasm. Paul and Mary found it difficult to think of anything beside the catastrophe they'd left behind. The freak fire that had consumed their home, which was the reason why everything they owned was new. Their jackets, their boots, Nick's knapsack with CANADA emblazoned on it, the books and crayons it carried. Life itself was new—it was the most striking possession at hand as they sailed forth—to be lived in a cottage on the coast of Vancouver Island. Side expenses would be covered by freelance consulting Mary hunted up in Victoria. And Paul would spend his time taking care of Nick. The main goal was to recover. To reconstruct some sort of routine for themselves while the house in Toronto was being rebuilt.

All this marked Nick as the odd man out. He was the pioneer among them, the freewheeler in their little clan. He'd lost the least, and the house fire, for him, was not a part of a larger, nastier tangle of his own making. In fact, the burnt house was the first bad turn in an otherwise unmarked life. Nick, alone, felt truly and freely overjoyed as the three of them stood at the front of the boat, laughing and calling to the birds and balloons.

Paul and Mary knew they were in deep trouble. What did you do when you knew such a thing? You said nothing about it out loud, because of the child. You ate puck-sized hamburgers in silence in the ferry cafeteria, while your son shoved handfuls of ketchup-smeared fries into his mouth. You flipped through the local paper, half in interest and half in amazement that so much was going on back home in Toronto, to no end at all for those on the west coast. You went to the washroom, if you were Nick's father, and sat down in a cubicle to pee, so you could look at the door and rest your head in your hands and breathe.

Mary fell asleep shortly before the boat docked on the

big island. Paul let her rest until the last minute, till there was no one left on the deck but crew. Then the three of them got into their rental and pulled off onto the roadway. Nick couldn't say enough about the view he had from his car seat. He swung his head from one side to the other, shouting, "I have such a good view!"

¶The house they had rented near Sooke was hard down by the shoreline, so close that even on hot dry days the garden hardly needed watering. The coastal wash blew up over everything, turning the greens and flowers into a glimmering diamond field.

They had chosen the house in part because it was close enough to Victoria to give them access to the city. And they had only to head up the coast to Long Beach if they wanted to leave everything behind.

Nick had a bedroom up in the rafters with a dormer window that looked out at the water. His habitual night-time drama of resistance to sleep came to a sudden end. At first Paul and Mary thought this was because he was being lulled to sleep by long days on the beach in the sun. But once, when Paul poked his nose in after midnight, he found Nick awake, his knees on the dormer window seat, gazing out at the night.

"Nick," Paul whispered

Nick turned to him.

"What are you doing?"

"Sleeping, Dada."

"What do you mean you're sleeping?"

"Sleeping on the water. See?" To prove he meant what he said, Nick lifted his small palms, signaling that this was the most obvious fact in the world.

"Okay," Paul whispered, and pulled the door shut.

❡Their new neighbourhood had its share of charming oddities; in particular, a little caravan of 1970s-era trailers on the edge of a nearby meadow. The trailers were patched with bits of board and plastic sheeting, and their roofs bristled with rusting, flapping tinpot chimneys. Whenever they drove past, Nick and Paul would play at guessing who lived inside. Nick put his money on a troupe of circus clowns, while Paul suggested day workers from a nearby organic farm. As they passed the caravan, Nick would call out for the car to stop.

"I wanna see there!" he'd cry, pointing into the cottonwood and scrub that surrounded the trailers.

Paul would laugh, saying next time, while Mary eyed him from the passenger seat and shook her head.

One afternoon, Paul caught Nick trying to sneak across the meadow. He'd made it twenty yards into the bush before he spied a grass snake and started shouting, "Dad. Dada! Over here! Snakes!"

They agreed to visit the caravan together. They knocked on a few doors, and found a group of the trailer dwellers using the back of a rusted, de-seated Ford pick-up as a hammock. The caravan, it turned out, housed a leftover community of hippies and their wannabe hangers-on, kids from Victoria and Vancouver and farther north who came with their Marine Band harmonicas, out-of-tune guitars, copies of the collected work of Jack Kerouac, their piercings and pot pipes, to stay until something else came up. The little caravan was the late sunset of the summer of love, and Nick was instinctively fascinated. The ragged gear and outfits, the spare dogs and chickens that shambled over from nearby farms, gave the place a distinct circus atmosphere.

Nick announced that he had a "harnonica," and that he could play too. "But it's at the house."

One of the young women offered to take Nick back to get it.

"He's just saying that," Paul said. "Or he thinks he has one."

The woman introduced herself. Her name was Mirella, and she offered to show Nick around.

Nick bounced on the tips of his toes. "Can I, Dada?" he crowed. "Can I?"

What followed was an interminable jam session, built around Neil Young's "Down by the River." Nick was given a harmonica and he honked and puffed along with grandly imperfect timing. He marched in a circle, lifting his knees high, pumping his free hand in the air. Paul sat with his back against the old rusted truck. The teenager beside him solemnly strummed the song's two chord verse for what seemed like half an hour. At one point, Paul made his way into the scrub to pee, and found himself laughing out loud at the sounds erupting behind his back. He thought he recognized these young people as latter-day versions of himself from fifteen years before, so he didn't bother to tease any of them out with conversation. He expected that their urge to get back to the garden had its best expression in the sunny, guitar-jangly early records of Joni Mitchell and Neil Young. They would feel, as he had in 1972, that their two patron saints had betrayed them. Why, they would wonder around late night campfires, pulling on some of the world's most fragrant marijuana, did those two have to go and become Americans?

❡Mirella fell hard for Nick, deciding that he was her own private angel. Every few days she crossed the meadow to their house by the water to say hello. She knocked on the door—studiously avoiding the doorbell as if it were spooked—and when Paul opened it, there she stood, in her denims and straw hat and Converse runners.

"Can I say hi," she would ask, "to your Nick?" Sometimes she stayed to play, and, with seemingly endless patience, listen as Nick chattered about his day. He picked up her favourite words and used them at each opportune time. Dinner, he would say with perfect upbeat sincerity, was very bogus. After his late-night tooth brushing he'd rub his lips and sharp little teeth, announcing, "Mm. That toothpaste is posh. It's so posh. And bogus." The new words were like a set of tools, but Nick had yet to figure out what job they were meant to do.

Mirella was long, lean like a boy, with straight yellow hair below her shoulder blades. She said she had run away from her family's house in Shaughnessy, but that her parents were "cool with that." Her family was originally from the States. There was some eastern money in her background, and the father had come north to Vancouver with one of the big banks. They had a second family home on one of the Gulf Islands. He'd tried his hand at a raft of west coast micro-economies: wine-making, candle-molding, cabin construction, even EST for a short period in the 1970s.

Mirella never mentioned a mother. Since she'd been on her own she'd had her share of underground jobs. She'd toiled for minimum wage—better, she pointed out, than what was on offer in the U.S.—in health food stores, dance clubs, record shops. In a guitar store in Victoria she'd learned to play a bit, and took some of her pay in stock—boxes of unsold strings and a slightly dinged acoustic. She had a collection of harmonicas, and now and again brought one with her. She would sit the boy down by the beach and play him a breezy twelve-bar blues.

"Do you like that key?" Mirella would ask. And Nick would nod and insist it was "his key."

Eventually, Paul and Mary put Mirella to work as a babysitter. There was no phone at the caravan in the woods, so Paul trekked across the field to check if a particular afternoon or evening suited her. The answer was almost always yes.

It was Mirella who introduced Nick to the local public library. Set up in a renovated Craftsman bungalow, it was another of the neighbourhood oddities lost in time. With no budget to speak of, it had managed to maintain a nice little collection of aging children's books. Paul liked the fact that the island library lacked the fluffed up, super-optimistic stuff they feed kids nowadays. Instead, there was Doctor Seuss coming out of your ears, old mystery novels, and a huge bin of Leonard Bernstein LP s—music appreciation for toddlers and adolescents. Nick found his way to the Maurice Sendak selection, which was complete. The greatest hits and the unfairly forgotten. Nick's favourite among the latter was called *The Sign on Rosie's Door*. The first time he brought it home, the book took Paul by surprise. It was about kids older than Nick, who lived on what looked like a block in Brooklyn. It was unlike anything his son had seen or heard about. The book had chapters—some short and others well-developed, almost short stories in themselves—portraying Rosie's antics. In them she comes off as a benign Pied Piper leading her more naive sidekicks. One of Rosie's games is dress-up, along with her friend Kathy, whom she nicknames Cha-Charoo. Together they mount a mock-Broadway performance for their friends, whose grand finale will be Rosie's rendition of "On the Sunny Side of the Street." Children who weren't New Yorkers could not dream up anything like this: Rosie standing on a folding chair, decked out in one of her mother's sloppy, off-the-shoulder gowns and a big befeathered hat, readying herself to sing the song from start to finish.

There was much more in *The Sign on Rosie's Door*, and Nick could not get enough of it. Every time he visited the library he would gather four or five books—about trains, or trucks, or cats and dogs that knew how to play the harmonica—but Rosie was always being returned to be renewed, until the rules made him leave it behind, to be borrowed on their next visit. Luckily, it seemed that no other child in the area knew Rosie existed. She awaited Nick each time he looked, like the most attentive of friends.

In Paul's mind, Rosie became an inhabitant of the Island, just like themselves. She lived at the library, and Nick had arranged a holiday for her at their house by the water. The book lay most often on the living room coffee table, but sometimes Rosie came upstairs for reading before bed. On long sunny afternoons she sat on the picnic bench in the backyard. Sometimes Paul flipped through Rosie on his own. The story struck him as familiar. But why? He was sure he'd never read it as a child. Did the cozily drawn streets of childhood Brooklyn remind him of his own New York youth? He couldn't see how. His family had not, as far as he could remember, visited Brooklyn. His father's life was centred on Manhattan, where he worked, doing something undescribable at the stock exchange. He was a jazz lover who haunted the clubs in the Village and the West Fifties. He'd left when Paul was eight. When he was ten, Paul's mother moved them to Toronto, which meant his memories of an American childhood were few. His dad, he seemed to remember, cut the front lawn wearing suit pants and a white shirt, black leather shoes shining in the arc of flying trimmings.

The car he drove was a hundred feet long and fifty feet wide. Once—Paul was certain about this—his father had exploded at his mother for suggesting that he read his son a bedtime story. I've got better things to do, his father shouted, than read that kid his baby books.

¶One afternoon, Paul was on his own down by the water. Mary was off food shopping. They'd arranged for Mirella to pick up Nick because Paul had plans to clean up the yard. But he felt too lazy and put off getting started. It was a perfect blue coastal afternoon, the sun and breeze so mellow they could not help but act like a drug. Paul lay down on the grass, his palms together under his head, and fell asleep.

When he woke abruptly an hour later he sat up and watched the sea. It swept in quietly, waves softening to foam a few yards from the edge of the yard. It wasn't long before Mirella would bring Nick back. Paul looked off across the meadow, half expecting to see them, a hand-holding pair against the backlit trees. But there wasn't a soul in sight.

With nothing else at hand, he reached for *The Sign on Rosie's Door*. It was the last book he'd read to Nick that morning and it lay open at a drawing of Rosie on her folding chair, her back to the reader, ready to sing. The dress, found in her mother's basement, had slipped from one shoulder to reveal a girl's jersey underneath. Built for a much longer body, the waist of the dress hung well below her hips. On her head was a big old-style hat—a kind of exaggerated fedora—with a band on the crown and a feather sticking out of it.

Something stirred inside as Paul gazed at the drawing. There was, he thought, in spite of his effort not to, something sexy about Rosie. And this seemed to have something to do with the way the drawing called up a memory of an older, lost self. Then it came to him.

He padded downstairs to the basement and fished around in the suitcases they'd yet to unpack. The bags were filled with things they'd begged from friends and family as stand-in mementoes of their past, to replace the things they'd lost when the house in Toronto burned. He found the photo album they'd pieced together from copies of photos they had sent to people when Nick was tiny, along with things Mary's parents had dug out of old boxes and sent to them. These mailings had sustained them in the months after the fire. In Paul's case there was no one he could ask for back-up photos of his own childhood. He had no family resources to call on beyond what had gone up in flames.

Paul brought the meager photo collection outside and sat on the grass by the water. He quickly found what he was looking for. It was a picture of Mary as a girl, posing in a dress-up outfit like Rosie's. The too-elegant, slightly revealing dress, the extravagant out-of-style hat, a boa and elbow-length black gloves. The similarity between this young Mary and Rosie was uncanny, almost scary. Was this some archetypal fantasy shared by imaginative little girls? Somehow—was it only dumb luck?—Nick had found his way to someone else's version of a young girl's fantasy, just like his mother's.

Paul meditated on the snapshot of his wife as a girl, and remembered, for a moment, how it felt to be very young, too young to know what it could mean to have your picture taken standing on a folding chair, in your mother's clothes, with your back to the camera.

It was almost six. Dinner time. In some loose islandy way, Mirella was often late returning with Nick. This irritated Mary, but Paul rarely worried. Now, something made him want the boy. He put on his sandals and started across the meadow that bordered the property where the caravan was camped. The undergrowth was brittle from lack of rain and it popped and snapped beneath his feet.

As Paul approached he heard Nick's voice. He stopped beside one of the beaten down trailers, feeling the heat radiating off its metal siding. It was topped with a chimney that smoked fragrantly, and a pile of fallen branches that shifted in the breeze. Paul thought he could smell them, the sweet and sour scent of broom.

Nick sat between Mirella's crossed legs. In his lap was a book, which he looked into intently, as if he were reading it. This was not possible, but the way his listeners paid attention made it clear that Nick was reporting the book to his audience from memory. Reading, for him, was just that—remembering out loud. He moved rhythmically, patiently, turning one page after another. The circle of young people shifted around him on the grass, smiling, quiet. The kid was doing his thing—entirely unselfconscious and spontaneous—the way a flower opens, regardless of who is watching.

Paul looked past them into a picture of what his son might become, what, as he grew, he might disguise himself as. But there were too many other things in view—the trailer, the trees, the sun cut like an orange behind them—for anything distinct to take shape.

On their way back to the house Paul held his son's hand too tightly, talking on about how he loved him. The day's surprises made him say it in too fierce a way. Not far from the house he came around in front of the boy and knelt, holding his two slim wrists.

Did he know how much he was loved? "Do you understand, son, how much?"

But Nick did not understand. He was still back with the circus people, reading from memory, or wished he was. His father's outburst made him call for his mother.

"Where is she dada? Do you know?"

They made their way across the meadow in silence. The house was dark, and Paul had no desire to go inside. He knew that Nick's mood would turn if he just let him be, so he hung back as the boy walked to the shoreline. It took all his strength to stay silent as his son bent at the waist and thrust his hands deep into the water. Nick pulled them out to see how they looked dripping wet in the light, then he pushed them back in again.

THE OLD WOMAN

Near Nick's daycare there is a hole a block wide and four or five stories deep. One day a building will fill it, but for now it's just a hole. A long steep track runs into it from the street. Dump trucks and diggers lumber up and down in the rising dust, looking like great monsters in a children's book. On Thursdays, around 4:30, just before the guys start to shut down for the day, Paul picks up his son and walks him over to the hole. The two of them hover by the driveway's open gate, at the lip of the hole. Along the curb stands a line of idling trucks that wait to haul away their loads. Sometimes Nick's mouth hangs open, or his lips round in a perfect moist o. The hole's effect on him is awe, the deepest regard and interest in the details of the dig. How many dump trucks? Which are full and which empty? What's in the full ones? And what will the men do with the enormous granite chunk they've uncovered in the hole's centre?

Nick pronounces his play-by-play, pointing one small finger at the dust.

Look! He's digging!

He's backing up!

Dumping!

With repeated visits Nick's father has become intrigued himself, though he pays attention to different aspects of the project. The predicted finish date, for instance, is long past. The back-and-forth of the trucks makes a mess that has spread for blocks. It hangs in the air, a curtain of brownish haze. And there is the talent of the workmen for living up to a stereotype, as they whistle at passing females with an almost priestly insistence. The men, Paul is sure, feel obliged. There is no desire in their eyes as they watch another behind slide by. Just the instinctive, competitive need to join in.

When they first started coming by, Nick would cry—deep blubbering tears that he brushed away with two hands—when Paul tried to move him along.

No! I wanna stay. Watch the hole!

But now he understands they'll be back. So they agree it's time to go, and Nick cheerily waves goodbye.

Bye hole! See you.

In Nick's not-yet-four-year-old view of time—a thing of little interest to him, aside from the fact that a day can grow late, and the moon will come out—next Thursday hovers comfortably into view. Its distance is something he can accept. Next Thursday, in his mind, is just another word for tomorrow.

But this week, having watched one dump truck load after another disappear into the city, Paul explains that they won't see the hole next week.

Why? I wanna stay! See hole!

Because next week they will be on an airplane, headed west, and won't be back till the weekend. The hole will have to wait for them till they return.

It is against all sense to give the boy advance notice about this, the missed hole Thursday, but Paul must take Mary into account. She will have Nick over the weekend, and there will be the usual questions: What is your father up to? What will the two of you do next week? It's Paul's firm policy to avoid any suggestion of secretiveness, between himself and Nick, and, even after months apart, between himself and the boy's mother. He would rather have things out in the open. Then their discussion will be about his plans and not about whether he's made them without talking to her.

He can already hear Mary's take on his plans to go west. Why, she'll ask, did he have to take the child anyway? At the end of fall to the Prairies.

Any travel plans might provoke an argument, but Paul's decision to take Nick west will raise a particularly contentious issue between him and Mary. Why, she'll want to know, did he need to take the child to see the old woman? After what they'd decided, and the way things had gone, wasn't everything best left as it was?

The decision at stake was made before Nick was born. It came at Mary's insistence, and was in fact a kind of quid pro quo: Paul could no longer remember what he got out of the deal, but Mary's end of it was that Paul's grandmother—his mother's mother, now in her seventies—would be kept on the outskirts of the child's life until he was eight. Their logic, as he remembered it, was that by then Nick would be older than his grandmother had been during the war, and so, could view a child's war-time experience with something like maturity. It seemed a cruel deal, but Paul decided to live with it. His grand-mother had had a huge influence on him, especially after his own father abandoned their family. It was she who had talked his mother into moving them up to Toronto from New York. For the past five years she'd been out of range, living with a niece, far away in a small western city, having moved there to escape the damp Toronto winters and to outrun her own loneliness.

His grandmother, Paul says, resembles a nearly extinct species, or a model of car whose original numbers are so depleted that when one runs by, it stands out as the last among the last. She is European born; a Canadian since the late forties; a Yiddish-speaker living out a second life in the Queen's English. Paul showed me a picture of her. A lean, aristocratically erect white-haired woman in a blue housecoat, her bony hands resting at her sides. Paul edged a finger over the photo to point out arthritic knuckles. And her hearing is going. She is hopeless on the tele-phone. If Paul asks how she is he learns that she needs to pick up celery and a quart of milk. Had I ever, he wanted to know, known anyone who lived entirely in the past? I thought of my parents. I didn't know my grandparents, all of them English-born and unwilling to follow their emigrating children to Canada. My sister ended up in

Melbourne. She might as well have flown to the moon. And though our childhood home had an oddly lifeless quality, this wasn't because of any particular interest in the past. Both my father and mother were Christian Scientist accountants who made a fortune on IBM stock in the 1960s. In my family, overt opinions were avoided at all costs. We ate dinner in polite silence and my father and I shook hands good-night, me in my pyjamas, both feet on the first stair up to my bedroom. I don't remember any books in our house, except Mary Baker Eddy's self-congratulatory latter-day Bible, which sat collecting dust on a living room end table. Every few weeks the cleaning lady picked it up and gave it a shake to resettle the dust.

Paul's grandmother lives in the past to the strictest degree. It is as if she is a monk and the past is the site, the temple of her devotion. In her Alberta room hardly anything is new. It's been furnished with things saved, mended, pulled from storage lockers, the leavings of her prior home. The TV is remote control-less. The couch brocaded, and the throw pillows tasseled. The art on the walls strictly generic—offering the kind of landscape you find at a furniture store along with the couch, as something colourful to fill blank space.

When Paul's grandmother lived on her own in a rambling brick three-storey full of boarders on Toronto's Palmerston Boulevard, she was unfailingly industrious: a baker, a soup maker, a bird broiler, and scourer of all things soiled. At Passover she cleaned not only the curtains and walls, but the ceiling, using a rag tied to a mop handle. She did the things all her neighbours had done, back when the surrounding streets were Jewish. In the end, she was the last one, all her compatriots having moved north or checked out, to enter that great chicken-plucking venue in the sky. When she finally sold the house—receiving a miraculous windfall in Toronto's overheated market—and packed to move west, Bloor Street was a carnival of new exoticisms. Korean cookies, KFC, and the gaudy porno outlets where there had once been family cinemas.

For Paul's grandmother, the only enticement offered by the present was her family. Every development in Paul's life was of interest to her, especially the great-grandson she had never met. Nick, in her mind, was tantalizing. Since his parents' divorce, she had maintained a campaign to have him visit her new Alberta home. "I'm happy here," she told Paul over the phone. "Let him see me happy." Birthdays and spring breaks were suggested, then vetoed by the boy's mother. No matter how many times Mary said No, Paul returned with another possible date. He believed it was important for his son to see, while he still could, the particularity of his great-grandmother's everyday; the industriousness of her old-world homemaking; her dedication to things that have become urban cliches, but once had the hard, inescapable, daily character of breathing: soup making, washing on the line, apples in a bag for baking. Once upon a time—as they say in children's books—you built a life around these.

Finally, they settled on Halloween—the first one when Nick would be old enough to go trick-or-treating and understand what he was doing.

It's warm here in October, Paul's grandmother promised. And then, of course, there was one more thing. Paul's grandmother was a survivor of the Warsaw Ghetto. As a child she was spirited out of the Ghetto in a trunk, drugged into silence, family jewelry sewn into the lining of her Persian lamb coat, currency in her hat band. It was this image, Paul believed, that Mary could not bear. It was nightmarish, Mary insisted, to put such images into a child's head.

While they were married, and even after, Paul held to their agreement. He rarely spoke to his son about his great-grandmother. He made a point of calling her only after Nick was in bed. But more recently this pact stopped mattering. With his time with Mary over why was he obliged to honour the cruel marriage-bound promise? Only the world's biggest sucker would do so.

❨Paul wanted to go west for a number of reasons. Toronto, where he'd always been happy, had begun to irritate him. He had far too much time on his hands, even for a single father. He wondered, deep in the pit of his gut, what he would do next. Sure, he would raise Nick. And raise him and raise him, until the job was done well. But would he do this in Toronto? Or some place quieter that was better suited to the job? He had fine nostalgic memories of Vancouver, and even wondered what it would be like to raise Nick in some college town in upstate New York. They could make day-trips to Manhattan as if it were a circus built for kids. These were things he didn't discuss with Mary, because they would introduce a new minefield around the issue of how to share their son.

Paul resented having to call down to the studio to make an appointment with Mary, as if he were a stranger. After their breakup she'd made her way into broadcasting, tired, she told him, of the pressures of immigration work. All he planned to say was that he was going to take the child west to meet his great-grandmother. He feared the old woman's time was running out. Anything could turn things upside down. A slip on the sidewalk or a bad spring cold. This meeting was the least he could manage, because soon enough, all there would be to see was a grave.

Mary squeezed Paul's visit between two studio interviews. Her assistant informed him that she had fifteen minutes to spare for him.

He sat in the chair where guests sat, with the big mike in his face and the headphones before him on the table, waiting to be put on, as if their conversation would not work without interpretation or translation. Paul got down to business. He told Mary he planned to take Nick west.

"Why?" she wanted to know. "Why now?"

"I want him to meet his great-grandmother. At least once. Nick can take it from there. It could mean something to him or not."

"You know him," Mary said. "He'll eat her up. Like he does everything else."

She was right about this. That's the kind of kid Nick was.

As they finished their discussion, if you could call it that, Mary did something that Paul, once he was on his way, couldn't get out of his head. She stretched—one of those cat-stretch yawns that involves the whole body. It reminded him of how at home she was in her body. The ability to uncurl and resettle without missing a beat. That was the mother of his child.

Alberta was unseasonably warm and blue. They drove the rental car south from Calgary, and as soon as the Rockies appeared outside the car window, Nick was overwhelmed by their size, their whiteness and startling nearness. On the passenger side of the car, where Paul had set Nick's car seat, the boy's hand rested on the lip of the door, fingers pressed against the glass, his head twisted to the right where the mountains paraded like one hundred trucks at work, trucks full of snow and slate and forest pine. As Nick saw more, the rough line of towering points transformed, in his mind, into a monumental choo-choo.

See choo-choo! See choo-choo!

For the last half hour of the drive, father and son were a great mad whoop-up act, a traveling circus celebrating the mountains as locomotives, the shorn fields before them as the world's greatest rail yard.

The visit, after all its lead-up, was banal. Paul and Nick

sat in their cousin's living room. Nick laid out his toys and then gathered them up again. They drove to the mall. They went to look at the little university that sat astride the deep windswept coulees, which had been carved by glaciers millennia ago. Paul's grandmother was not overly outgoing with Nick. The back-story to their visit was too strange; the sudden appearance of a great-grandson she'd never seen. It was as if she were trying to handle him lightly, because his appearance was in some way magical, and an overreaction might cause him to evaporate—poof!—like a puff of smoke.

In turn, Nick was careful and quiet around his great-grandmother. When he and his father were on their own he said two words again and again as he bounced on the tips of his toes—Greadgranmommer, because it was difficult, and Bubbie, because it was easy.

No one spoke of drugged children in suitcases traveling the Warsaw underground like underripe potatoes. On a couple of occasions Paul saw his grandmother from across the room with a look in her eye that seemed to say, Something needs to be said. But each time she let it go, and the conversation drifted toward trivialities—the forecast and what Nick would eat for dinner.

Halloween became their focus. Nick and his great-grandmother scrounged in the basement for the ingredients of a costume. Since they were in the west, she informed him, he should be a cowboy. They found a red check kerchief, a pair of purple gumboots that fit him with socks stuffed into the toes, and a corduroy vest in need of some work to get it down to size. The neighbours promised a cowboy hat. When the father of the boy who lived next door rang the bell, he held out an entire ensemble: a pint-sized straw hat, a leather holster, and a gleaming silver six-shooter, so detailed that both child and great-grandmother mistook it for the real thing. Laughing, their neighbour placed the child-sized hat on his head, cocked the pistol and pointed it at his skull. The sound when he pulled the trigger was like a door latch catching.

Click. No gunfire.

This struck Nick as hilarious. Like a clown act from heaven.

Halloween day was warm and bright, with the smell of leaves and cut grass in the air. By dinnertime, storm clouds were piled in the west and the air had grown cool. Nick refused to wear a jacket over his costume, so Paul dressed him in two shirts and tied the kerchief as much like a scarf as he could manage. There was a quiet argument between Paul and his grandmother about the gun. But Nick cried when he was told to leave it behind. The outcome of their negotiations was that he would skip the holster and carry the pistol, as they might in Texas, hidden in the bag where he collected his candy.

Nick flew along the broad suburban lawns, running up to front doors and standing before them, his pillowcase in hand, as if simply appearing was all it would take to coax the homeowners to open up.

Trick or Treat! Paul called from the bottom of each lawn, and the front door would open, light flaming around his boy.

When they had visited fifteen houses on one side of the street and had begun working their way back along the other side, Paul suggested they had enough candy.

"No!" the boy insisted. "Not yet!"

At this moment, as Paul entered the familiar zone of disagreement and tried to think of the simplest way to escape it, a gang of kids swept around them, laughing and yelling. One threw an egg, which clipped the top of Nick's hat, knocking it off. Before Paul knew what had happened, they had snatched the pillowcase full of candy out of Nick's hands. Paul heard them laughing as they sprinted up the block and disappeared behind a bungalow.

Nick was too startled to cry. It was as if, as a Halloween novice, he thought this might be part of the night's entertainment.

They stood, robbed sad suckers, at the bottom of an expanse of prairie lawn. Paul coaxed Nick along. As they made their slow way, hand in hand up the darkened street, the storm that had been building broke. Fat drops, as big as soap bubbles, fell through the glow of the street lamp and burst on the pavement. Nick raised his palm to the cold rain. When they'd reached the covered porch they sat and watched the storm tear through town. Rain drummed so loudly on the shingles above the stoop that neither of them heard the door open behind them.

Paul's grandmother looked out.

"It's over, the rain?" She looked past them into the dark. "In Warsaw, in autumn, it rained like this. In the parks the flowers would lie down flat, as if asleep. And the soldiers gathered under the trees. I can still see the way their cigarettes glowed in the darkness."

Nick looked up. "Gun is gone," he said sadly.

"I have something to say about this," she said, "if it's okay with your father."

Paul nodded that it was.

"Did you know, Nick, that every man and woman was once a child?"

Nick thought about this, then nodded tentatively.

"And as they grow older, in everyone remains the pleasures—not the memory—but the pleasure of their childhood. The body and time cover it up. This loss is a great tragedy. Who can say how great? When someone points a gun at a man or a woman, he points it at the child that once was." To this she added, "Farshteyst?" In Yiddish the word meant, quite simply, Do you understand?

The talking stopped. Nick blinked once, baffled. What he'd heard had a familiar tone, not unlike the books his father read to him before bed, but there was something mysterious behind the lesson he was being offered.

"Okay. So. Goodnight." The door shut behind them.

The boy's hand lay on his father's knee. Together they watched the rain jump in the street. It ran in the gutters and dripped from the leaves in the yard. On the wet pavement the lights of distant traffic flared before the night swept in again, a dark underwater green.

THE SUMMERS FATHER WENT AWAY

Paul says, "There are people you can talk to about certain things, and people you can't."

We sit in a city park in the shade of a heat-strangled maple. Behind us his son plays with a boy who shares his name. The two Nicks chase a mangy squirrel around the swings, up the slide, only giving up when the animal breaks for the street and scoots beneath an idling bus. Then they settle down to a project in the sunbaked sandbox.

Tucked into Paul's knapsack along with Nick's things—his juice cup, his books, his sun cap, which he should be wearing but continually tosses on the ground—is a battered copy of J.D. Salinger's *The Catcher in the Rye*.

"I just finished it for the fifth time," Paul says. "I don't follow the gossip about Salinger's hideout in New Hampshire, eating vegan and drinking his own piss." It's Holden Paul loves, and Manhattan, along with the bit players, the cab drivers, doormen, and all the cranks and youthful troublemakers. "But I'm done with it. Five times is enough. I know parts by heart." He begins to recite what I vaguely remember to be the book's opening, and holds it out to me. "Do you want it?"

In my hands the novel seems to have no weight at all. It's like holding a bird or a balloon. I read Salinger when I was a teenager but it had no real impact on me. New York City. The Museum of Natural History. And the narrator's arch, knowing voice. What did any of it have to do with me? I sensed something familiar near the end, when Holden and his sister lose something—was it a record album?—in Central Park. And I understood how it might offer Paul solace from the demands of parenting. It gave him someone else's family to think about. Someone else's precocious kid to sympathize with. I wonder, too, if Salinger's Holden Caulfield struck him as the kind of enfant terrible that his Nick might grow up to be: smart, capable of great, spontaneous humour, but infinitely sad about the world and the end of childhood in a way that no one would ever change.

Something about the way I set the book down irritates him. He picks it up and tosses it at a metal garbage pail chained to the end of our bench. The book sails, pages flapping, through a crown of bumblebees that are undeterred by the city-ordered garlic deep inside the pail, the stink of which is meant to ward off pests.

The book lands in the dirt. We stare at it where it lies, converted abruptly into trash. A pigeon alights nearby and eyes us in that side-of-the-head pigeon way. It moves close enough to pluck bits of the cover for its nest.

"Books are dead," Paul tells me, as if to pronounce Holden's eulogy. "It's true. I know, you'll say they still make millions of them. And people buy them." Had I, he wonders, flown on a plane lately? The fact is I hadn't, so he informs me that the only thing being read on board was the newspaper—the ones they give away for free. That is, when people stopped fiddling with laptop spreadsheets and the little movie screens in the back of the seats. "Books," he says, "might as well be our telegrams. Our typewriters and 78s. These things got ditched because they were one-upped. They worked fine, but hardly anyone wants to make time for such stuff once something faster comes along. Teachers don't even bother with books anymore. The computer is today's instant meal. You open one the way housewives used to open a can of tomato soup." He let's this hang in the air, but then there's more. "Childhood," he says, "the way we knew it. It's finished, too." He stares at the book on the ground as if daring me to pick it up. "Hardly anyone has time for it anymore. It's not popular to say so. And when I do, people look at me as if I should shut up. When, they seem to wonder, will the government build a prison for people who talk the way I do?"

Paul's soliloquies do not require my agreement. All he needs is a good listener. More often than not I don't have an opinion about whatever is concerning him. I'm no expert on these things. I'm a childless loner. But I've found a certain satisfaction in knowing Nick, his peculiarities and the openness in his child's ways.

"Can it be," I ask, "that things have changed all that much? It's hit or miss, isn't it, from family to family? From one mom to the next. From one city suburb to the next. They aren't all simply parallel universes—the same TV channel playing simultaneously on different sets."

Paul stares at the book in the dirt for a long time. He smiles sadly as the pigeon breaks free with the whole cardboard cover.

"No," he says, "ours is a dark time. Cold and tense. Fixated on speed and gain." And then to prove that things were different once, what do you think he tells me?

His father loved him. Back when parents still had time for their kids. It's true, he admits, before I can remind him, that his father cleared out. Abandoned ship when Paul was eight. He remembers the night his father did not come home. A casserole was baking in the oven. It smelled cheesy. Oniony. One of those childhood smells that makes the whole world seem right. Someone should bottle that smell, he says. A Stanford grad student should go to work on that. Get a grant from Kraft or Procter & Gamble and go in search of cheese and onion casserole, circa 1968, cooked in a Westinghouse range using New York State power at 4:45 pm. People would buy that in a can and spray it around whenever they needed a little homey feeling in the house.

Paul and his mother sat down to eat the casserole at half past seven. She'd let him play in the yard until then, wacking away at the weeds with his baseball bat. But it was getting on toward bedtime. He swears he remembers it all like it was yesterday. Better than yesterday. At nine he went to bed. When he woke up the next morning, sun pouring in around his canvas window blind, he heard his mother crying in the front room. She wore the clothes she'd had on the day before.

"Oh," he says, "it was shit then." They both hated him. They waited a few weeks, then took his father's suits to the Sally Ann. His hats too. Some derelict must have walked the Bowery in style after that drop-off. They emptied his writing desk into a tin garbage pail.

"I managed," Paul says, "to sneak a few things for myself. When I look back now, I don't know how I had the courage to grab them from under my mother's nose." A pair of gold cufflinks engraved with his initials. In a carved wooden box he found the spare keys to his car and carried them with him all the time. With childish ingenuity, he thought he might one day see it parked on a street corner. Without a moment's thought he would get in and drive away.

That, Paul says, would teach his father what it felt like when something you loved simply vanished, as though it never existed.

These are Paul's worst memories.

But there are others. The ones that make him certain that the father who left loved him.

"First," he says, "I remember the way he kissed me, with his full lips. European lips. He would purse them—is that the right word?—and moisten them, then kiss me full on the lips. I remember his eyes as he did it. They were open.

It was casual, an acknowledgment that I was his boy. At least that's how I see it now."

What else can he offer as evidence that he was his father's beloved?

Everything his father owned, he says, was his. When they drove by a property his father had just bought, they would stop out front long enough for his father to say, That's yours. It belongs to all of us.

This lack of possessiveness, Paul believes, was his father's way of making him feel he had responsibilities. Or at least, it was an effort to signal that they were on the horizon. This was his father's forte. Other fathers might talk to their sons about sports or women or hunting or dogs. His father, he says, viewed him as a kind of equal. And when Paul did something his father disliked, a dislike telegraphed with a look, the disappointment was killing.

Now, Paul says, when he looks at his son, he sometimes feels, in some imagined but half-real way that he knows how his father felt when he looked at him. This worries me. It doesn't seem fair to Nick.

When I first met them there was all-round joy in the house on Shaw Street. Paul and Nick were whooping it up like sailors on shore leave. Having Nick led Paul to move out of his rented apartment and set up house in perfect bohemian splendour in a converted bakery on Shaw Street, between Harbord and College. Paul bought the building from a guy who'd knocked down walls, even some ceilings, to turn the place into a huge open space, a kind of house museum devoted to his collection of Harley Davidson motorcycles. When Paul and Nick moved in, the space smelled of motor oil and hot chrome. The floors were a perfect invitation to Nick to ride his tricycle through the front room, roll up to the service elevator and bang on the call button, then ride into the elevator and press the button for his father's room on the second floor. There, Paul could be found standing in the light by the front window, his Fender Stratocaster slung over his shoulder, playing the same three chords again and again. D A G. Sometimes he varies the order and the rhythm, but for the most part he believes in these three chords. F and B were useless. They just interfered with what you were trying to play. Once, he did admit to me that E and C, at just the right spot, have their usefulness.

Their home is bare inside. Paul's goal, it seems, is to make the place into a child's refuge—safe, unadorned, unencumbered. No family photos on the wall. No drawers packed with the past. No TV acting as a portal to the outside world. After the divorce, the furniture went to Nick's mother and Paul never bothered to replace much of it. He picks up milk crates and wooden boxes in the neighbourhood's alleyways, and uses them to store books and CDs. A big easy chair and a couch collect dust by the front window, and an old wooden kitchen table with two creaking chairs stands at the back of the room. In the basement there is a highchair and the crib Nick used until he was two, but beyond that, no baby stuff. The walls are white, freshly painted, and the maplewood floors have been sanded and stained a buttery yellow, so that when the sun comes in the big front window the space sparkles. It blazes at midday and glows at evening. Sometimes Paul wears sunglasses to read the newspaper.

Out back, behind the garage, is a deck with high red brick walls, which, when it had a roof, was part of the original bakery ovens. When the previous owner bought the place he removed the roof and power-washed the brick walls so they were soft as felt. On hot days the deck is a little kiln, taking in the city heat and holding it till evening. But on cool days it's an oasis where Nick drives the toy cars that are his obsession. His most precious toys are a collection of old American convertibles—three inches long and an inch-and-a-half wide; just big enough for the details of each model to look accurate; the lean bucket seats on the '66 Thunderbird; the humped trunk on a '49 Buick; the hips on a '70 Cutlass. The cars travel in a shoe bag with an elastic drawstring and sleep beside Nick in his big bed. The convertibles had become an irrepressible point of connection between Nick and his father, and the back deck's wooden slats serve best as roads, bridges and tunnels.

After these, Nick's great enthusiasm is music. He has a stereo in his room, and when I visit he invites me up to listen to the Beatles' *Yellow Submarine* or some kids' CD he's been given as a birthday present. When his father puts music on in the front room, Nick hovers nearby, knowing he's not to fiddle with the stereo dials. But once the music begins, he asks, What that it's called? He listens carefully to the answer, repeating it in order to remember it. The most unpronounceable selection is fine with him. Abdullah Ibrahim, he says, the syllables a bit stiff and showy, but correct. This is Abdullah Ibrahim, he confirms, head nodding, one small hand flat on the table, fingers flapping up and down with the rhythm.

But these things don't begin to describe the boy. I doubt I can really bring him across to you. His excitement, his curiosity, his smile impossible to put into words.

❨It had not yet sunk in for Nick that his mother would not be joining them. Ever. I suppose Paul did not go to great lengths to make this absolutely clear. So, each day was like a holiday. A dawn-till-dusk vaudeville act. Just the two of them, because, as Paul said, with his marriage at an end, he didn't care to see anyone if he didn't have to. Just the boy. He seemed to be trying, however difficult it proved to be, to erase the past entirely. To go forward, from the day he and Nick started over together. I met them around that time, just as father and son embarked on their new life. I became a kind of accomplice. An old car guy willing to babysit the two of them. What Paul needs is a willing listener, nothing more. He has no interest in my advice regarding the boy. And when he invites me to dinner that means he wants me to cook. My answer is always yes. I live alone, in a bachelor apartment with a view of a back alley, and I eat at least one meal a day in a restaurant on Bloor Street. This routine has its charms—

 I'm a ghostly regular, a fly on the wall in the coffee shops and noodle joints. I might well be part of other people's cast of neighbourhood regulars: that guy with that old black car who eats alone with the newspaper. I've always been a kitchen lover, a cookbook collector and herb grower, and it is my good fortune that Paul's home contains a gleaming, restaurant-quality kitchen renovation left by the house's previous owner. Cooking at Paul's house is wonderful. Out the big window over the sink there is a view of the rooftops and fence posts of his downtown neighbourhood. It's a typical Toronto view: brick walls and cockeyed garage doors and elaborate white-plaster shrines dedicated to Portuguese saints.

There is one room, at the back of the basement, over which Paul failed to take control. As part of the sale agreement, the previous owner promised to empty it, but hadn't bothered to follow through on this. Paul was in the house a few weeks before he looked in and discovered the room packed to the ceiling, its dark cement walls invisible behind the stacks of abandoned junk, a narrow walkway clear down the centre of it all. He put a big brass padlock on the door to keep Nick out, intending to empty the room's contents and have it trucked to the dump. But before he got around to it, what might have been expected to happen happened.

I was in the kitchen getting dinner started. Paul, as far as I knew, was upstairs. When I last saw Nick he was out back playing with his cars.

But I was wrong about the whereabouts of father and

son. Paul had taken a beer out to the yard where he slept in a deck chair, head back, mouth open to the sky.

The boy had abandoned his cars and found his way downstairs. There, as if by magic, the mysterious door his father refused to unlock had fallen in on itself. The padlock held, but the hinges had rotted through and the door was flipped up on its corner. In the light falling from the bare basement bulb Nick had wormed himself in.

What was in the room that dada had never opened? Newspapers piled to the ceiling. Empty suitcases. Decades-old cans of diced tomatoes and jarred pickles. A busted piñata. A pyramid of near-empty paint tins, displaying on their bent lips the dark hues Paul had painted over when they'd moved in. Stack after stack of ruined paperbacks, yellowed, waterlogged, hobo-smelling, as if they'd been stored in a leaky boxcar for decades. The best proof available that Paul was right about one thing: these books were the deadest of the dead, their authors entirely forgotten. Strangest of all among these things was a fireman's uniform. When I found Nick he was half into it. One boot on, the hat tipped back on his head, the canvas coat like an outsized cape over his shoulder. He looked at me, radiating simple joy. The costume was his greatest discovery. It turned him into a fantastic figure. One of the heroes who, along with policemen, ambulance minders and airplane pilots attract a child's instinctive delight. That evening a struggle began. Nick wanted the fireman's uniform in his room. He lobbied for it to be tucked into bed beside him, and then said it could hang in his closet.

 But Paul would not stand for either of these. The uniform stank, he said, which was not entirely true. It was old and damp, he said. It was garbage.

The child was inconsolable. It was his fireman, he wailed, as if the uniform contained a man, a hidden hero he'd freed—a boy's version of Snow White—in the basement.

How could dada do this to the fireman? Nick wailed, as if he were being denied his closest friend.

They arrived at a compromise. Paul hung the uniform in the garage. The boots stood, heels against the wall. The jacket hung from a nail that jutted from an oily crossbeam, the hat on a shelf above the nail. This set-up pleased Nick, though to Paul the outcome looked like a lynched man. Whenever Paul agreed to unlock the garage, Nick ran out to see if his "man" was okay. He put stones and handfuls of grass in the pockets of the jacket. He took off his shoes and marched around in the boots.

Paul hated these antics, but he could not think of a way to end them. He imagined an elaborate lie in which the uniform was stolen. He even daydreamed about burning down the garage in an act of sheer desperation, and he might have done it if the building hadn't shared two walls with neighbouring garages. Before any real firemen appeared he would have burned down a block's worth of rattletrap buildings.

Week by week Nick's infatuation grew. It overflowed and attached itself to policemen. Passing emergency vehicles brought him to a sudden stop in order to raise a hand in salute. He told anyone who would listen that he had a fireman back home in the garage. Would they like to come and see?

This disagreement heralded the end of the honeymoon on Shaw Street. Like an argument between married people, it had no rational underpinnings. Nick instinctively loved, while his father instinctively hated the city's servers and protectors. This wasn't the first time they disagreed, but it was the first to cause true dissent, a sort of proto-rebellion, which Paul struggled to contain. It made him feel lonely, he said, as he'd felt when it was still unclear whether it would be himself or Mary who would take on Nick full time.

As if to fill his head with something other than his child's current obsession, Paul was beset by a recurrent dream. It returned nightly, becoming more hallucinogenic and strange after any prolonged argument about the "man" in the garage. In it, old cars were the main players. It included no people beyond Paul himself, who found himself in the midst of an undetermined errand. Suddenly he remembered he'd left a '62 Pontiac in a downtown parkade. What followed was always the same: sudden recognition; a specific abandoned car (one version had recurred so vividly that Paul now half-believed that he had actually abandoned a light blue early sixties Ford Fairlane in a downtown parkade). The dream's pointlessness might have been funny if not for the way it was blanketed in anomie and directionless mystery. Did it mirror the arc of his intermittently aimless life? Or did it echo the breakups—

the disconnection and loss—that haunted his childhood and now his own marriage? Whatever the dream meant, it confirmed a gulf between father and son. Nick collected and loved his little convertibles. They were his friends. They slept safe on his bed. Paul's dream cars were like bait, lost loves, bits of himself he could not recover.

❡Paul tells me that life used to have a different smell. Sharper. Narcotic. Roof tar steaming on a rain-soaked morning; the dark spice of grass cut at sunset; brewer's yeast—flowersmelling, oversweet—wafting above a bridge full of traffic; broom, geranium and caragana, the perfume of his youth.

What he seems to want for the child is that there should be no falling off of these smells and the feelings bound to them. But everything—everything—conspires against this. I think of Paul's claim to know, when he watches his son at play, how his father felt looking at him when he was a boy. This is another impossible leap—over time, and across the boundaries of the most fundamental loss. When he tried to explain these feelings to Mary she waved them off as nothing more than his usual ghost stories. Save that nostalgic stuff for your friends with their heads under the hood, she'd advised him.

"Ah," Paul says. "It's bad stuff." How had it happened to him? Hadn't he steered himself clear of these sorts of disasters? Apparently not. All he wanted for his son was solidity. Stability. If he could shield him from his own rootlessness, his wanderings and self-doubt and regret, he'd be happy. The boy, lovely and naive, was still untouched by it all. His own life, Paul knew, had a tumbleweedy quality to it. The Levittown youth. The disappearing dad. The move to Canada, as if he and his mother were summering birds looking for a safe point to land. His mother's early death and then his rambles west. A kind of hiatus from it all during his years in Vancouver. Those years had a quality to them, of rest, of peace and sense. When he thought of them now he felt sad that he hadn't stayed, though he had no idea what he'd be doing if he had. If he had never met Mary. If she had never convinced him to move east. The day they drove away from Vancouver he couldn't talk. Not one word. Because if he had he would have bawled. So they drove east in silence. Once they'd reached Revelstoke he loosened up enough to say he needed to use a bathroom.

This rootlessness, the unpredictability and accommodation that followed each uprooting, went far, far back in his family as if they had a gene for it. A special predilection, the way some do for disease or baldness. His father was one of those tragicomic suburban men who show up in *New Yorker* short stories. But even before that, his father's father's life was something out of Hansel and Gretel—the Jewish version, if such a thing exists. Green Mendel the Practical Joker was his grandfather's nickname in the central Polish town where he lived. Paul had no idea what was green about him, but he did know that Mendel was the community mascot, the town scamp. He changed what he did for a living from year to year. For a while he was a newspaper agent. But when the train finally came through and his customers found they could subscribe by mail, they did, to avoid dealing with Green Mendel. He was the only Jew in town to join the volunteer fire brigade, and in this, too, he was a kind of mascot. The brass helmet with its visor down to his nose and the grey belted jacket gave him the air of a Jew masquerading as a non-Jew. The effect was so entertaining he found himself elected the band leader—a sort of glorified majorette for the fire brigade's brass band. To complete the picture, he was also the town's amateur philosopher. The only premise of his thought passed down to Paul was this: Green Mendel assured anyone who listened that if he'd had the opportunity to create the world, each man and woman would live for five thousand years. Each day they would become a little younger, until finally, they would dissolve into nothingness and disappear in a puff of smoke, which, according to Paul's father, had happened to green Mendel one hot late-summer day. He vanished abruptly, as if the wind had taken him. With Green Mendel gone, what remained of the afternoon? The smell of overripe plums in the air and the spectacle of storks on parade in the field.

Paul's inheritance consists of things that suddenly slip away, and he swears he will end this pattern when it comes to his son. One result of his effort is irritation at any threat of events outside his control. The appearance of the fireman's uniform in the basement room full of dead things and disguises—Nick's "man" in the garage—had exactly this effect.

As the summer winds down Paul's neighbourhood grows quiet. The worst of the heat is over and the road crews pack up their make-work projects—their pyramids of orange pylons and madcap glow-in-the-dark hats and vests. The grass in the parks is dead brown for lack of rain, and the first leaves of fall gather in the gutters. If you give Nick a broom he sweeps them out of the gutter, as if to gather them back for the trees that lost them.

Nick has grown more serious. He and his father squabble over trivialities. What to wear and what to eat. What time to go to bed and when to get up. When a police car or fire engine passes, eliciting hops and shouts, almost somersaults, Paul edges as far from Nick's antics as he can, making it clear that he will not, can not, could not ever possibly care about such things.

I am amazed that a child can be such a formidable competitor in argument, on the questions that arise from a day's routines. And I don't understand how deeply Paul's fears run, how the life he has made for the two of them is like a river over which hovers the rumour of flood, until one day when we pick up Nick at his daycare.

We make our usual slow way home, up alleyways and across parched gardens on the sunny side of Shaw Street. Nick directs us here and there, suggesting we backtrack and revise our route. If we were to follow his directions we would arrive home by nightfall.

It's seven before we unlock the front door.

The phone rings just as I've got dinner started.

Nick picks it up. Drops it. Then stands at the bottom of the stairs shouting up to his father. "Dada! Phone!"

I hear Paul's side of the conversation from my post at the stove. I stir my sauce and watch a pair of crows fly down and strut along the back fence. They seem to listen, too. Paul speaks in a normal voice at first, but quickly becomes angry and raises his voice louder than I've ever heard it.

"No. I won't come down tomorrow," he shouts. "If you want to interview me you get over here now! You've got the address, right? Don't give me that. If you know my number you know where I live. Get down here. I'll wait for you."

Paul is too furious once he's hung up to explain who the caller was. His son is overwrought with curiosity. Who was Dada yelling at? Using his words, as they call this sort of behaviour at the daycare.

Paul gazes out the big front window. His son kneels on the couch and looks at the street. Together they watch as a police car double-parks in front of the house. Paul cranks open the window and places Nick where he can see outside.

"You sit here," he says. "Listen. I'll be using my words with these guys. Okay?"

I take Paul's place on the couch. Nick and I kneel side by side, our elbows on the windowsill. The cops look cowed as Paul approaches. The bigger of the two wrings his hands, and the other puffs up his chest as if to do a kind of mating dance. They look like two guys who know they are doing the wrong thing.

Paul begins to shout almost immediately.

"You tell me what she told you! She saw me reach into her car? Well that makes no sense. I know the car. It was a shit brown Celica with ripped black vinyl seats. I glanced inside because an open window in a parked car always strikes me as odd. I thought: open window, bag on the seat. That was it."

One of the cops signals to Paul with his raised palms that he should calm down. But this just revs him up. At this point Nick emits a tiny, worried, "Dada," his hands small on the sill, his eyes locked on the scene unfolding before us.

"So she must not have liked the look of me. That's all. Because she has nothing else to go on. Am I right? Right? So what are you two doing here?"

The answer to this is obvious and a little funny: Paul ordered them to come right over.

One of the policemen walks back to their car and picks up the radio phone. He talks on it while the other says something I can't hear.

"Lie detector!" Paul shouts. He sounds as if he might burst. "Are you crazy? No, I won't come in and take a lie detector test. What for, for Christ sake?"

At this point, the two cops have had enough. They

 give Paul the flat-handed cool down signal. They mumble some policemanly advice I can't make out. Then they get back in their car and drive off.

When Paul comes back inside, Nick has already shambled up to his room and shut the door. He's had enough mad shouting. He doesn't understand what he's seen and, uncharacteristically, doesn't want to.

Paul sits on the couch beneath the open window, cursing. He holds his head in his hands, gets up and paces, then flops back down again. Some old-timer reported her pocketbook stolen. That's what the cops had called it. A pocketbook. The woman said she'd seen him near her car, called in a description, along with the licence plate of his car, which she'd seen him get into. The cops didn't seem to believe Paul was their man but they were checking things out to be safe. But why did they call first? This drives Paul crazy. Since when did cops call to tell you they wanted to talk to you? He curses and shouts. Nick stays up in his room. Maybe he is down on the carpet, getting a new angle on his little convertibles. Or he might be plunk in the middle of his bed, arms up over his head in the loose-limbed sleep of the young.

What was it about the scene in the street that made Paul so angry? I'd never seen him shout, even when Nick had to be asked ten times, twenty times, to sit on his chair and eat. Was it being mistaken for a thief that had touched a nerve? If those cops had pushed it, even the slightest bit, Nick would have seen his father driven away, shouting, in the back of the cruiser.

The street turns soft evening orange behind the window. Paul and I sit in his front room. Neither of us bothers to turn on a light. As the street darkens, the room is lit by the glow of a street lamp.

"I wish," Paul says, "that Nick hadn't seen that stuff with the cops."

But you let him see everything, I think.

We sit awhile in silence. Paul on the threadbare couch under the window, through which Nick watched the afternoon drama. I on the floor, my back against the wall. As I often do when Nick is not around, I feel as though I have no real reason to be in the house, that the man seated before me is a stranger, a familiar face I pass on the street. But my urge to look out for the kid is strong.

Paul crosses his arms over his chest.

"I've told you," he says, "how my father disappeared. Well, that sort of thing happens. I embarked on my little life. And that might've been the last I heard of him. But life has its twists. We moved to Canada, for a simpler life. That's what my mother told people. But I think she feared my father's reappearance. In Toronto we were far enough away for her to feel safe. You know, I ended up a music writer by chance. I just fell into it. For a few years it was fun, covering the big conductors and arena rock shows, and even the underground stuff. It meant a lot of traveling. I went to Manhattan a lot. On one visit I went walking on the Lower East Side. I'd never seen that part of New York City, and I was interested. I passed a window on Rivington Street. It was a knishery, one of the holdovers from the old days named for the guy who'd founded it. In the shop window—no lie—I saw my father's face. At first I kept on walking, but I made myself turn and came back to the place. I confronted the face. But like most things in my life there was an undercurrent of the ridiculous. The face turned out to belong not to my father, but to a cousin of his, a guy a decade younger, who shared the same melancholy Russian eyes and ruddy cheeks. I'd not seen him since I was a kid. The guy was friendly. He didn't seem all that surprised to see me, as if he'd been sitting there waiting for us to reconnect. He said my father was still in the city, that he'd declined after he left us. He told people he was working, but in fact he was no more than a fringe figure in the neighbourhood. He showed up at student marches. He fancied himself a kind of local do-gooder. Once in a while he got his name in the *Times* for preventing a mugging. The most spectacular instance of this was a recent rampage by a lunatic who had stormed into a restaurant, doused the diners with lighter fluid, and then began flicking a barbecue lighter, threatening to set them all ablaze. My father's luck—he was passing outside and saw what was going on. He slipped inside the place, jumped the fool with the barbecue lighter, and held him down till the cops showed up. For a week or two he was a hero, but soon enough he slipped back into the anonymity of his Loisaida tenement room where he boiled eggs on a hot plate and bathed in the big kitchen sink."

Paul's father's cousin told him that if he hung around long enough he and his father would cross paths. But this was someone else, surely. Who was the man talking about, this derelict hero and Bowery clown? Paul headed for the uptown subway, finished his business in the city and went straight home.

¶ Paul closes his eyes and listens—I along with him—for the sound of a sleeping child. From far off in the city we hear a siren blazing toward us. It is the sound of the boy's night dreams: help is on the way, heroes in big-brimmed hats and canvas coats would spend the night, if need be, extinguishing the apparitions of Green Mendel, of Rivington Street, of bungalows abandoned on suburban evenings.

DREAMING OF CRANBROOK

This is the story of Paul's last big trip with Nick. They went west and then south in search of Paul's cousin Bernard. I felt a little lost without them. I wondered, if they were gone long enough, would Nick return changed, with a new way of talking and a different look in his eye? While they were on the road I paid unerring attention to my clients. My accountant's office on Bloor is near a pharmacy and a grocery chain outlet. People wander in with their shopping in their arms, desperate, hopeful, their tax receipts in a paper bag. This is how I met Paul and Nick. Paul had questions regarding inheritance that I had to read up on, and when my rate proved surprisingly low they invited me to dinner in return.

The week they went in search of Bernard my old car went cold as stone. It was as if the thing had been alive, carrying some spark from the day it rolled off the line, which had been extinguished. As I watched the tow man pull it down the street and out of sight the phone rang. Sure enough, it was Paul, on the road, with an update.

Bernard Altschul was a talk show story waiting to happen, the kind of thing they air and end up depressing everyone, from the dead-end guest himself, through the audience, who stare, wondering why, and on up to the host, the producers, the executives—Manhattan moguls with million dollar everything, now the slingers of some sad sack's life as product. Bernard never did make it onto TV. He was though, from time to time, in the papers, on page six, page eight, unless at the time of writing he was residing somewhere small enough where his difficulties rated front page news. Paul didn't know about Bernard's track record in the media when he first went out looking for him. A gun possession charge, probably trumped up, had been detailed in the back pages of the *Detroit Free Press*. A conviction for soliciting was pending in Denver. The one incident that made the Canadian papers took place just over the Montana border in Alberta, when the RCMP stopped a van Bernard was riding in. The driver came up on their computer with a drug record, so the border agents strip-searched everybody, kept them in a cell overnight, interrogated them as though they were Mexican drug kingpins, and only let them go when the drug sniffing dogs came up empty. In the world of crime investigation there is one absolute: the drug sniffers do not lie.

Paul never did find out when Bernard started drifting. Was it as far back as the fifties? Was Bernard a beatnik before anyone knew the word? Or did he drift out into the sixties haze, a straight arrow with a blank future, lost in the crowds of newly minted hippies? Paul believed it was a mama story. The mother, he told me, was at the root of Bernard's strangeness, his absolute resistance to joining the world in any conventional way. She'd made him feel unloved. How Paul knew this, I don't know, and I wondered if this explanation revealed as much about Paul's troubles as it did about Bernard's.

If Bernard's wanderer's urge was a mama story, it was a doozey. He simply could not stay put. Sometimes—if things were particularly comfy—he would stay in one place through the course of a couple of seasons, say, fall and winter, picking up work on a city road gang, or as part of a landscape team, raking leaves and putting down bulbs in suburban beds. But he always moved on, leaving a trail of people who knew him just well enough to remember that he was polite. That he kept himself clean and neat. That he never spoke a cross word, and could sit, silently thinking over a cup of coffee for two hours. For all his strangeness, there was something about him that attracted sympathy. Once they pushed past the first discomforting impressions, people who met Bernard fell for him. They felt obliged to look out for him, to buy him dinner or sit patiently while Bernard talked on about people he could not forget who'd "done him wrong," about the windfalls he'd spent in a week or two, about the times his mother "went crazy and forgot she had a son."

Paul was drawn into Bernard's life by indirection and coincidence. He'd heard very little about his cousin when he was growing up, so Paul had little family feeling for him, but he had his own inclinations toward indolence and misdirection. You couldn't be his friend for long and not see those inclinations.

When Paul received the first call asking if he'd be willing to help find Bernard, he was intrigued and agreed to try. Yes, he could pick up and leave town at a few days' notice. He liked the prospect of rambling drives through the American wilds, from the sprawl of Detroit to the Montana bluffs.

Once he'd collected on the sale of his father's car collection, Paul went on what he and Nick called "Permanent Vacation." He claimed not to miss his work as a music critic. He said he'd fallen into it without intending to. He even blamed it on his own father. Some dads begin with baseball, or bicycle rides, or wrestling. With Paul and his father it all began with Thelonious Monk. When the family was new—Paul just five or six—they lived near New York City, in a commuter neighbourhood, one of those Levittowns full of identical bungalows and fresh suburban dreams.

On rare nights, when Paul's mom was out with friends at a movie or playing bridge, his dad would put him in the back seat of the big Cadillac convertible, with the massive canvas top rolled back. They would drive into Manhattan on the leisurely post-rush hour roadways. Once in Manhattan, they would thread the uptown and crosstown streets with no apparent aim. Paul's dad laid his arm across the front seat. He whistled old-time tunes—"Get Me to the Church on Time" and "Just a Gigolo." He chatted with pedestrians as the car idled at a red light. On these outings Paul felt that his dad forgot he was there at all. The whistling, the chatter with passersby, none of this was for his sake. His dad wasn't the sort of man who acted cute for the entertainment of a child.

Once in a while their rides had a destination. They would make their way through lower Manhattan and park near a jazz club in the Village. The club was a big thing in those days. If you went there, you knew what was really going on in the city's music scene. Once they'd found a parking spot, Paul's father would put the top up. Paul remembers sitting with his head back, watching the span of metal and canvas cover them and shut out the night sky, the stars, the block of buildings above the car. Then they went inside, into a dark room where men played loud discordant music. Of course Paul can't remember much about what this music sounded like. His father would buy him a Coke with a twisty straw, so he could watch his drink do somersaults on its way to his mouth. If Paul grew tired he lay down on a banquette, clutching a napkin or a swizzle stick, until he slept. In this way his father would listen, while Paul slept, to the late sets, which were played especially for the maniacs, the uncompromising aficionados, insomniacs, night birds and musicians with no other life beside the clubs.

What must it have sounded like to a five- or six-year-old? Like the clatter of a subway train as it crossed the bridge over the river. Or like the time an uncle of Paul's brought his old Ford over to their house and blew the engine when he went out to start it, having neglected to put oil in it for months. But a child is interested in noise. He doesn't resent its intrusion. Nick's that way. When he gets hold of a toy that makes noise, he's elated. He makes it make that noise, and then shouts, It's very noisy! as if he's discovered gold.

Paul says he knows, too, that he and his father must have talked as the city flew by—the bridge, the tenements and office towers—but he has no recollection of what they spoke about. He remembers that a street light they routinely passed didn't work for weeks, and that a cop directing traffic had a sandwich tucked into his tunic pocket. He remembers wondering what sort of sandwich it was. But what he and his father discussed, he cannot say. What he does remember is that during a stretch of 1964, when the cop directed traffic beneath the burnt-out street light, there was an unusual act on the stage at a club called the Village Gate. The performer went by the elaborate name of Thelonious Sphere Monk. Sphere, the news magazines said, because he was no square. Paul's dad hated this guy. He hated the way he chopped at the piano keys with his elbows. He hated the way he'd arrive an hour late for his final set. And most of all, he hated the big bear dance Monk did when his sidemen soloed. It was a weird slow funky bear-groove, arms akimbo, butt wiggling slowly to the swing of the bass, a hand up to the hat brim, a kind of slow, sly salute before Monk returned to his piano and began to cut the weird blues chords that were like a careful explosion in a clockworks factory.

On one of those nights, as Monk bearwalked over to

where Paul and his father sat, Paul's dad, ever so carefully, slid his big shoe out in the aisle and tripped Thelonious Monk. Monk rolled, careened, blasted over a table full of finger-popping beatniks and came to a stop by the booth at the front of the club where they collected the cover charge. The whole room went silent. Music broke in mid phrase. Waiters froze with trays full of glasses aloft. Conversation went absolutely still. And then came the big mad tinkling laugh of the pianist as he pulled himself up and continued out the door of the club to the street and was gone, leaving his band to finish the set, and to wonder if their leader planned to return.

A couple years later, Paul's father disappeared. The fiasco at the club seemed funny at the time—a blooper destined to become a good party story. But as time passed and Paul's life proceeded in its own tumbleweedy fashion—what he sometimes referred to as his long discreditable bohemian adventure—he began to wonder if everything could be traced back to that moment: his father's shoe in the path of Thelonious Monk; the crescendo of silence that preceded the wreckage and laughter and the show's star tumbling out the door into the street.

¶I would venture that the worst thing about finding Bernard is that it has made Paul lazy. He had a job, a wife, a life, not to mention Nick, when he got his first call from Eugene—Eugene Konstantin, that is, Bernard's great-uncle in New York and Paul's cousin however many times removed. In each case the pitch was the same: "I'll stake you. Find him. Bring him back and I'll help him get straight." This is Eugene's standard line. Eugene issued the itinerary and Paul picked up and went. One winter it was Detroit. Then a hot month in Alabama. And next, holed up for weeks in a picturesque little motel on L.A.'s bowery.

It was never entirely clear how Eugene, from his Manhattan roost in the east Eighties, knew of Bernard's doings in Nogadaches or Boise or Denver. His knowledge seemed to rely on a combination of things: Bernard staying in one place a bit too long, and, in a few cases, getting himself into trouble. With trouble came press coverage. But most importantly, where there's money there's a way. Eugene likely had someone monitoring the news and the police countrywide, because if Bernard made the local paper in a midwestern logging town, Eugene knew. Once, he'd discovered that Bernard was using a food bank in Madison. Paul wondered if there wasn't a detective out there—his own dark other half—who scrambled after these bits of information, while he was the one Eugene sent to do the road work. Paul was the net employed to scoop up the lost man and bring him back for retooling, to make him suitable for what Eugene liked to call "normal life." Why, Paul wondered, had Eugene chosen him? Did he recognize in Paul the soul-weariness required to coax a broken-down case out of his cave?

Once, as Paul was getting ready to head off on another round of Bernard hunting, Eugene convinced him to come down to New York City. What he had in mind was a kind of first class send-off for the relative-for-hire. Paul took

Nick to New York with him, and they stayed in a hotel near the Forty-Second Street library. It offered children's videos as in-room entertainment, and had a full-time cappuccino dispenser in the common lounge. Paul arranged a sitter through the front desk—one of the staff, off duty, who liked kids. When he left, she and Nick were cozied up on the big bed watching "The Ice Storm" on TV, Nick's mouth open wide as Toby McGuire slid across a darkened field of frozen grass.

"Whatsat?" Nick asked again and again, pointing at the screen with pleasure and fascination.

Eugene had somehow got wind of the fact that Paul loved music. So he took him to the opera. The opera of all things. Beforehand they went out for a meal that must have cost more than a month's rent in a small Canadian city. There was caviar and smoked sturgeon so silky you felt bad putting it in your mouth. Then on to the entertainment. A four-hour opera based on *Sophie's Choice*. Brilliantly costumed performers singing their heads off about Auschwitz. Eugene and Paul were seated centre orchestra and it was less than an hour into the program before Paul began to feel that he would lose his mind. He was overcome by what he called that Edgarallanpoeurge to leap to his feet, throw his arms in the air, and scream at the top of lungs. He held tight to the arm rests and thought: No. No. No. Don't do that. DO NOT DO THAT. At intermission he broke for the street, hoping Nick would still be up when he returned to the hotel. The baby sitter would have to find other company.

Paul understood that no one forced him to accept Eugene's offers to go in search of Bernard. He made a sort of free-lance job out of it. But finding Bernard wasn't easy. More often than not Paul missed him by a day or two, Eugene's information on Bernard's whereabouts being not quite fresh enough. Paul would return depressed, the trip a failure, having slept in umpteen bland motel rooms, and having talked with locals in one town after another, only to realize, too late, that half the people he met were covering for Bernard. This bought him the time he needed to slip out of range. Bernard gained the loyalty of small-towners. They remembered him respectfully, like a friend. Recognizing this proved depressing. Whether it was Rhode Island or Compton, wherever Bernard might be found, he had friends. Again and again, Eugene insisted that Bernard be uprooted, for his own good. Clearly, what Paul got himself involved in was an elaborate family abduction. The more time Paul spent finding Bernard the less he really wanted to bring him home. But the more he traveled in search of him, taking the ease of repeated free trips, the harder it became to say no to Eugene. Paul was hooked. He was deep inside Bernard's life and the rhythm of pursuit. He might see Bernard once or twice a year, for a couple of hours, but after Nick, Bernard was one of Paul's main fascinations.

❨When the phone rang after midnight I knew it was Paul. With his child asleep, he quickly became tired of listening to himself think. In the big hollow space they lived in he couldn't watch TV without waking Nick, and by midnight he was too buzzed on coffee to read.

"You awake?" he asked in a whisper, Nick's sleep at the forefront of his thoughts. "You see anyone interesting today?" This was a question to which he didn't necessarily want an answer. "How's business?" was another of these. "Any tax fraudsters walk in and shake your hand lately?" Paul could talk about anything after midnight—to knock as much of the night back before having to face the end of it, sleepless. And when he didn't have to concern himself with Nick's warm, sleep-filled body, Paul got around to talking about Bernard. It was as if he were talking about Bob Dylan or Saddam Hussein. Bernard made it into conversation in the weirdest ways.

I sat in my little kitchen at the picnic table left by the previous tenant, which stands in as my kitchen table, listening to Paul talk from somewhere in his gutted bakery, the phone as far as possible from the sleeping child. The two of us tethered across the downtown like night birds on the wires in the back alley, jawing at one another.

The driving, Paul insisted, was exhilarating. One trip took him across southern Ontario, late in the day. Nick slept as the sun set slowly before the car, gloriously golden on the snow and trees. The whole mundane countryside took on a magical glow. Dead-looking farms and ruined little outhouse buildings, rows of snowbound cars and trucks, the scrubby southern Ontario tree line, all grew more beautiful as the sunlight settled lower on the land. In these final few minutes, with the sun a fiery line on the horizon, the car full of its molten light, Paul felt he would cry, but the sight of Nick's sleeping face in the rear-view mirror, pitched sideways, the colour of prairie wheat, unaware of the blaze they were driving into, changed his mind and he laughed out loud.

In a little notebook they kept a list of the people they met. Just their names. No details about where they met them. It amounted to a rambling list of would-bes and could-bes. People they chatted with or sat beside at a restaurant who were drawn to Nick's exuberance and told them about themselves or the town they were in.

Tiffany Toth.

Toby Studebaker.

Spice Luck.

Echo Sunbear.

You couldn't make the stuff up.

They usually met someone if they stopped for a meal. They had a crazy act when they settled into a place—especially the kind of restaurant where you had to order standing up at the till. Nick would find himself a table, gathering the cutlery and napkins over to his side. From there he would call, Dada! And Paul would divide his attention between ordering and waving. Paul would raise one hand in salute. Nick would do the same. Paul would waggle his fingers in the air. Nick the same. And so it would go, like cut-rate vaudeville or a homegrown performance piece, while the other diners eyed them, wondering what came next.

Soon enough Nick would start a conversation with a stranger at a neighbouring table who, biting into a cheeseburger, would have to answer to the great philosophical query, Is that a cheeseburger or not? The metaphysics of a four-year-old view, somehow hanging on the excitement of contradiction. And then came the topper, which kicked off a rollicking roller coaster of conversational chaos: I'm not the person with the cheeseburger, you're the person with the cheeseburger. And on it went from there.

Now and again they left their car at the motel where they were staying and took a bus along some unknown route. When they were good and lost they'd take a cab back. Nick loves taxis. He views them as something altogether different from regular cars. Once inside he sits up straight, rubbernecking, mouth open, trying to see what's passing outside. Paul says he likes these cab rides, because suddenly you're stuck in a car with a local who tells you about the things only locals hear. The small-town cabbies are the best for this. Paul told me about one—this was in Wyoming or Illinois. The driver was a purple-turbaned Sikh. He introduced himself as Jas, short for Jasminder, and was anxious to take account of his hardworking people's accomplishments in America. As they skirted some outlying road he said he would call his mother. There was a short cell phone conversation in Punjabi, and the car slowed in front of a split level with a big picture window where Jas's mother stood, smiling and waving. They all waved back, and Jas's mom entered the pantheon of local characters who came home with them and lived on, like old friends they might yet see again.

The only figure in this cast of characters who made no impact on Nick was Bernard. He didn't seem to care who this unfindable cousin was, even though he was otherwise cousinless, with no siblings, not even a mom at home like most other kids. Bernard remained as abstract and unknowable to him as God. It didn't help that there were no up-to-date photos. Paul has one picture of Bernard, a square black-and-white snapshot from the late fifties with a real Lenny Bruce look to it. It is of a group of middle-aged people at Bernard's bar mitzvah in a Los Angeles synagogue hall. He looked like a normal enough kid. A little geeky. But lots of geeky thirteen-year-olds turn out fine. They learn to take care of themselves. They get good at one thing and go from there. One thing, it turns out, is enough to arrange a whole life around. What struck me about the photo was that the kipa Bernard was wearing—you know, the skullcap—was too big. And it seemed to glow. Everything else in the picture was grey. Men's suits, women's dresses, the cabinets in the background. But the big satin kipa on Bernard's head was on fire. It was moonish. Electric. Very weird.

As far as I know, Bernard broke with his mother in the late 1960s. Or she broke with him, embarrassed that her only child was a little touched, no mama's boy about to live out her ambitions for her by becoming a suburban model citizen. And then his mother died suddenly, before she got around to cancelling the trust fund she'd put in place for him when he was a child. Bernard didn't want her money. Instead, Eugene, who had power of attorney, made the withdrawals, and Paul ended up on the receiving end.

Which brings me to Paul's last trip in search of Bernard. It began with the usual call. Eugene from New York, directing Paul to a place of an altogether different sort of regional exoticism. Billings, Montana. Paul looked it up in his Webster's. "Billings (bil'inz) [after F. Billings (1823–90), railroad president] city in S Mont., on the Yellowstone River: pop. 62,000." He'd been given the dictionary when he was a teenager, which meant it was a good two decades out of date, so he tried a couple of travel guides. There was nothing there you could call information. Billings, the guides agreed, was a small North American city where the living was good—where slim couples jogged by the river and the old mansions nobody could afford to live in anymore were transformed, Cinderella-like, into lacy bed-and-breakfasts. One photo caught Paul's interest. It showed the city sunk in a coulee valley filled with fog, the summer green on its surrounding bluffs bunched up and rolling like thick shag rug.

"Nick is not so enthusiastic this time out," Paul told my answering machine before they went off in search of Bernard. "But I'm talking Billings up railroadwise, if only because its named for a railroad baron. We'll fly to Calgary and then drive south. I'll call along the way. To keep you up to date. Nick will want to say hi."

They went southwest as the summer shifted to fall. I went away at the same time, so news of their travels came to me via the answering machine, which I dialed into using a numbered code. Eugene had given Paul a cell phone—forced it on him really, telling him he wanted to receive a progress report once a day, whether they were sitting right next to Bernard and heading home, or just gazing into the sunset like a couple of desert dogs. I don't know if Paul behaved and called in daily reports. But when he had a free minute, if Nick was napping, or had found a park he liked with swings and a slide, or when they were just sitting, as Eugene put it, like a couple of desert dogs staring at the sunset, Nick with his juice and Paul nursing a cold coffee, Paul would call me at home. My machine collected at least an hour of his ramblings before the message tape filled up. Roadside calls with the roar of semis in the background. The sound of children yelping and laughing. Dishes crashing into the wash-up bin at motel diners.

They stopped in Lethbridge overnight. They ate Chinese food downtown, and for after dinner entertainment, watched two drunks fight spectacularly in the upper floor window of an apartment block, until one of them—or both, if they managed to collaborate—set fire to the room's sofa and heaved it out the window. This spectacle Paul narrated to me over the phone as they watched.

"Eee Hah!" Paul shouted as the sofa hit the ground and was engulfed by a second burst of flames. Nick thought this was the funniest thing he'd ever seen, and shouted EeeHah! all the way back to their hotel, interrupting himself only once to watch a lone early-evening drunk shuffle alongside the darkened downtown storefronts.

"You won't believe what the kid just said," Paul whispered into his phone. "He views this drunk. Then he tells me, or himself, Someone's learning to walk. And nods like he's just said the sagest thing ever."

Back at the hotel Paul insisted they take a bath. Nick fought and screamed until he was standing in the water, where he finally calmed down, warming in the dim shade of yellowy green light that fell from the cracked fixture over the sink. Paul turned his son so he lay chest up in the water. And there he fell suddenly asleep. Though the water grew cold, Paul let Nick sleep for a few minutes. Then he lifted him out and set him on the big quilted bedspread to dry off.

In the morning they followed their usual routine and went looking for breakfast. As they walked Main Street, Paul stopped at a smoke shop. Next to the Lethbridge daily he found a copy of the previous day's *Billings Gazette*. Its lead headline read: "Hit-and-Run Knocked Out of his Cowboy-Style Boots." Paul slipped the newspaper under his arm. They walked on to a diner where Paul ordered as Nick wandered the place, investigating every corner and peeking over the cashier's counter. He returned now and again to say he'd found a very dark house at the back of the restaurant, and that in all the coffee cups patrons were leaving their crusts. This was Nick's word for anything left over that you didn't really want. While the kid turned the place into his own personal funhouse, Paul opened the Billings newspaper.

Of course it was Bernard. The boots were among his few distinguishing features. Eugene wanted to buy him a new pair, but Bernard was proud of his boots. He didn't need a replacement. They'd been bought in Calgary, at a place called the Calgary Shoe Hospital on the Eighth Avenue Mall. The place was owned by a burly Jewish character who Bernard called real. That Jew, he'd tell Eugene over the phone, when he was explaining why he would not be buying any new boots, was the real thing. Bernard liked his worn-out boots. He believed they tied him to the rural settings, to the very landscape he rambled through.

Why, Paul wondered, had the headline writer insisted on dubbing them cowboy-style? What sort of journalistic bullshit was that?

Paul considered not telling Nick what had happened to Bernard. They could roll into Billings, make believe they'd gone Bernard-hunting, and then head home the way they always did when Bernard was unfindable: tired, ragged, and quieter than usual as they covered the miles they'd already seen, backwards, in their rented car. But once they arrived at Billings, Paul found this impossible. He wanted to know what had happened to Bernard, and that meant asking questions. In no time Nick had figured out that Bernard was gone. No longer around. Dead. What does dead mean to a child? Very little. Once, having heard the word, Nick came up holding a family photo, and announced, Dada, this picture is very dead. Bernard's death was the first thing about him that Nick took any interest in.

"Where is he?" Nick asked over and over. "Daddy, where is he? Why isn't he here? Is he here or not?"

The more they learned the worse it got. The couple that managed the motel where Bernard had stayed were flummoxed when Paul introduced himself as Bernard's cousin. They had never heard Bernard talk about family, and being sure that Paul must be more shaken up than he seemed, they offered to look after Nick while Paul lay down on their couch. Instead he called me, his voice eerily warm and deep as it was recorded by my machine hundreds of miles north.

"It's me again. Where are you? Did you tell me you were going away? I'm a little spooked, because of what's happened here. Are you okay? Nick and I are all right. We're visiting the motel people who rented to Bernard. You know, they're the type you don't really meet in the city. They'd talk all day if I let them, because they loved Bernard. That's clear. And they think I might be in some state of grief that will lead to further disaster. I haven't told them the truth about this. But I am a bit shaken up. I feel like I might know what it's like to be hit by lightning. They're in the front room showing Nick the TV. He makes like he knows all about it, and then he just sits and stares, giving away, you'd think, the fact that he's hardly ever seen one. Well. These people, the Macullums, they say Bernard walked everywhere he went. He walked into town and out of town. Those cowboy boots must have been comfortable. But whenever he walked alongside the highway he walked the wrong way. You know how we're always told as kids to walk towards the traffic? It's an instinctive thing—you don't want the cars coming up on you from behind. But Bernard just wouldn't play that game. He gave the drivers the opportunity to strike him down. He was testing his luck. Or he just didn't care. The Macullums call him their angel. Now that he's gone, they say they talk about him all the time."

Later that night two local policemen appeared at Paul's motel door. Word had gotten back to the cops that a relative of Bernard was in town. They were anxious for an interview. If nothing else, they wanted to tell the coroner what should be done with the remains. The cop said "remains" as if he meant to use language Nick wouldn't understand.

The identity of the driver of the hit-and-run vehicle had been discovered. The police had received an anonymous tip, which led them to a Ford pickup, parked in front of a mobile home on the outskirts of Billings. It bore the telltale damage. Nobody answered when they pounded on the trailer door, so they left a warrant and impounded the truck. When they returned it was to investigate a report of a gunshot heard coming from the trailer. Inside, they found the owner of the pickup. He was dead of guilt or just plain exhaustion and unwillingness to deal with the repercussions of what he'd done in a moment of haste and wild fear on the highway outside Billings.

Paul agreed to help the coroner arrange Bernard's burial in the Jewish cemetery. To pay for the plot he handed over Eugene's ever reliable credit card. But the hard luck didn't end with Bernard's funeral. The dead driver's Scottish girlfriend was cited for overstaying a visa, and without her partner's sponsorship was likely to be deported after living in Billings for more than a decade.

❡Paul didn't know how things could have ended up worse. Nick seemed to feel it too, and he sat, listless in his car seat, eyes wide, his attention elsewhere.

"I want to go home," he whined.

Paul had no idea how Nick figured out that they were not retracing the route they'd already travelled, that they were headed west and not north. Was it the slant of the morning light? Or did Nick simply remember some of the landmarks on the way down from Calgary that were not showing up? Had he secretly learned to read road signs? Regardless, it was clear to him that something unspoken was taking place.

"Dada?" was the repeated call from the back seat. "Dada? Why are we going this way?"

What Paul hadn't known how to explain was that Bernard's death had repercussions for them, too. Nick knew he was due to stay with his mother for a few weeks. What he didn't know was that she'd gone to a Michigan school to enroll in a summer training program. There was even the possibility of her being hired to teach radio broadcasting to the loafers and sophisticated misfits who were farmed out to Cranbrook Academy by their parents. Nick's mother had refused to forego her time due with him, even if it meant flying the child down to Detroit, where she would pick him up. This was the tentative plan. And Paul had grudgingly agreed to fly down with Nick, drop him off, then take a train back to Toronto to save on the return ticket. Now all that seemed senseless. With the Bernard fiasco at an end, why not simply use Eugene's rental to take the child to be with his mother? It seemed ridiculous to go home, only to fly back to Detroit and turn around again.

So Paul pointed their deluxe rental—air conditioning roaring—toward Michigan.

Nick knew something was up from the start. And he wasn't having any of it. When Paul called to describe this part of their travels he sounded worse than I'd ever heard him. Whispering. Halting. The cold tone of a man in a prison cell.

"He won't stop whining," Paul moaned into his phone and my answering service. "There's a tantrum every hour. First it's juice. Then milk. Then music. And heat. He says it's hot no matter how high I run the air conditioning. He's like someone else's child. Hateful and charmless and inconsolable. What have I done? Was it the impact of the death, or just the change in plans? Or the time we've been away, and he's just wanting his home and bed and familiar things? It's like we've never set out together before."

Of course, eventually, they made it to Cranbrook, a leafy campus surrounded by mansions on rolling hills of the real American prosperity. Paul thought of Bernard as they wound their way past the mock Tudors and faux chateaux. Would he have found a way to get by if his wanderings had brought him to this part of the country?

It was a quiet Sunday. They rolled through the Detroit suburbs, Nick finally asleep in his car seat, exhausted. Paul had the rearview mirror positioned so he could look back at the soft sleeping face. Along the way Paul had managed to lose the scrap of paper where he'd scribbled the phone number and house address where Nick's mother could be found. He couldn't even remember the name of the program she'd come down for. How, he wondered, was he going to locate his ex-wife in time to get himself back on the road to Toronto before dark?

It felt like the first afternoon of fall, the first hour or two when the air changes, the light gets thinner, and you notice that the breeze in the trees is bringing down leaves lightly, one by one, so that if you listen carefully you can hear each one hitting the ground. They parked the rental by the art gallery, and set off to look for someone who might be able to help them find Nick's mother. The summer student behind the information desk didn't know what to suggest. Maybe, she thought, they should check the married student dorms. People up for summer programs sometimes stayed there. She drew a little map, which Nick took over as his own, to show them how to find their way across the campus.

Paul and Nick took their time and more or less ignored the map. They wandered through empty department buildings and peeked through the glass-doored offices marked "History" and "Languages and Literature." It all gave Paul the feeling that another life had been out there when he was young, which he'd managed to miss, because his ridiculous father had tripped Thelonious Monk, bringing about all the semi-calamitous, wayward and wasteful things that followed.

They used the toilet in a sprawling basement bathroom whose tiles and porcelain reminded Paul of a Greek bath house. He lifted his son onto the outsize seat with their standard patter: I lift the boy; he directs penis; are you finished, Nick? They wandered into the college assembly hall, with its shabby, squeaking seats, and sat on the edge of the stage. Paul picked up a copy of the college hymnal. The school song was pasted on the inside front cover. It was one of those Hail to Our Alma Mater-type things that seemed to belong on a World War One battlefield.

The first dorm buildings they came across were brick, three stories high, built in a u-shape around a grass and brick courtyard. Inside they found a gang of stragglers who hadn't gone home for the weekend. Paul peeked into one room, where Alice Cooper blasted from a plastic turntable. An unwatched computer screen blazed blue and purple, and ragged beach towels hung in the window in place of curtains. Lying on the bed, his heels up on the wall, was a short, fat, buzz-cut kid who said he was from Virginia. His T-shirt read "The Sex Pistols: Never Mind the Bollocks."

Something about this scene made Nick cry. The quiet blubbering tears of a younger child coursed down his cheeks. Over Nick's cries for his mother, the kid from Virginia confirmed that the married student dorms were not far away, though the walk might be too much for a child. Paul cut his risks and led Nick back to the car. They stopped in front of a campus map. This would be their last chance before night fell to find Nick's mother, or Paul would be forced to take the boy back to a hotel to rest up before a second try the next day.

The dorms, as the art gallery clerk had called them, were in fact two-storey grey stuccoed townhouses surrounded by rambling treed yards. Their front windows overlooked a pond of circling ducks and geese, all of which seemed to be protecting a single white swan. And sure enough, in front of the last duplex on the road was Nick's mother's dented station wagon. It sat in front of a yard that had been planted like an English garden, with boxes of roses, red and gold dahlias, and big overgrown bushes of blooming phlox. It was a mess, but somehow it all worked. The garden's wildness was under control. Bathed in the late day sun, its colours were deep, almost too much so to be true.

The man who answered the door shook Paul's hand.

Too firm, he said later into my answering machine. Too goddamn firm.

But it wasn't just the handshake that made Paul feel sick inside. There was something about the garden—its careful chaos and wild beauty—that made him more fiercely aware of his own inadequacies. Never in a million years could he devote the time and energy it would take to turn a yard into something like that. Mr. Firm Handshake insisted on giving Paul a tour of the yard while Nick and his mother laughed and hugged and chattered in the kitchen. The backyard was a notch less brilliant than the front. The sun was going down in the trees, and since they had nothing to say to each other they stood and listened to the sound the breeze made in the leaves. Paul announced that he only wanted to bring the boy, that he would have to start back for Toronto soon.

It was terrible leaving Nick behind. It all felt like a bad joke. Maybe he'd sneak back while Nick was down there with his mom. Wearing a ball cap and a false beard, he'd watch from the duck pond across the roadway, pretending to rake trash from the rushes, just to see his son emerge in the morning. But you could get reported for that sort of thing. What if Nick saw him, weird-hatted, peering out of the bulrushes, and shouted Dada! It was the sort of thing the kid would do.

Paul hugged the boy on the doorstep. Nick gave his father a big open-mouthed kiss, and then they did their restaurant act: one waved, then the other, until Paul got into his car and turned it around. He coasted in the direction of dark skies in the east. The road dipped and rose. It skirted hills of deeply green mown grass. Near the final exit from campus a dark form appeared in the lane ahead of Paul's car. At first he thought it was a garbage bag, but as he slowed and came closer he recognized it as a Canada goose. It had been hit and dragged a fair distance. Paul stopped beside the carcass and gazed down at it through the open window. The body was big and the neck long and twisted, the bill hidden from sight. There was a cool silver sheen emanating from the bird's feathers, and skid marks that revealed the path of the accident. How had someone driven this road fast enough to manage the collision? What could they have been thinking as they continued to drag the bird along the pavement?

He was on his way. He would make Toronto before midnight. There, he would start again, almost like a child himself, his first autumn on Shaw Street without the boy.

ANYONE GOT AN E HARMONICA?

The last word to cross Paul's lips, shouted sharply at the top of his voice was, according to one witness, shitsack. But there were many witnesses—kids, working people eating a sidewalk hot dog, tourists up from Buffalo shopping for cheap T-shirts and mugs with Toronto logos emblazoned on them. One of these late-summer visitors believed that Paul's last word was, in fact, fuckbag, which, when reported to the investigating officer—a grey-haired grandad of a cop—elicited a wince. A hot dog vendor claimed, at first, that he was only aware of shouts coming from the street, and couldn't confirm anything specific he'd heard in the heat of the accident.

"Whatever the poor guy yelled," he said, as he slapped relish and sauerkraut and hot peppers on a slick wiener, "he yelled it loud." For the newspapers, later in the afternoon, he added: "If I had a choice, I'd say dirtbag. It makes the same point without the filth. You know what I mean?"

❡I can't say what motivated Paul to get his Jack Kerouac haircut. On first seeing it I thought it suited him—short in the back and swept up and away from the forehead. It was suddenly apparent that Paul was a handsome man, in an old-fashioned, seedy movie star sort of way. But there was something creepy about the change all the same. I had seen pictures of Paul's father, from around the time he'd walked out on the family. With the haircut, Paul looked like a trimmer, scruffier version of his dad. It was uncanny. But these things happen to a man as he ages. You see him in January when he still has youth in his face; you bump into him in September and everything's changed. The weight's come on, the hair's receding, there's a new pair of glasses obscuring what used to show brightly in the eyes. He's become his father. Or, to put it more flatly, he's become a dead man. For Paul, the haircut seemed to set him back and move things forward at the same time. He stopped looking like a holdout—a seventies leftover who had somehow never adjusted to the fact that the Weather Underground was dead. Still, the Jack Kerouac thing didn't feel right to me. I knew the father's trajectory. I knew what it had done to Paul and his mom when the man vanished into a summer evening, taking nothing but his car and Paul's beach toys, which had been left in the trunk after their last visit to Coney Island. At first, Paul—eight years old and completely unprepared for the disasters adult selfishness settle on children—fixated on the beach gear.

"When's daddy bringing my stuff back?" he would ask his mother over their tuna casserole or macaroni and cheese. Paul's mother would begin to cry, so dramatically and unstoppably, that the boy would forget his lost toys and concentrate on comforting her.

In the time I've known Paul he's not spoken often of his father. But when the subject does come up, it explodes onto the scene. There is an outpouring, a kind of emptying of memory. I sit, confronted by his obsessive monologue, feeling like a television interviewer whose guest has gone out of control. How, I wonder to myself, do I stop this guy?

Paul tries not to let his rambling reminiscences about the past take place in front of Nick. Anything else is okay: death talk; raucous drunken, or weed-powered storytelling. Nick has seen and heard it all. He is the camera recording his father's ups and downs. But not the old man. That Paul saves for me and only me, as far as I know.

It seemed, too, that with the haircut came more of the guarded recollections of fatherhood, as if, unconsciously, looking like his father made Paul think about the guy. He would pin me down late at night, after an evening of food and talk and wrangling to get Nick to sleep. It might be midnight, with both of us exhausted, and still, still, he'd want to talk about daddy.

In particular, I recall a night, not long after Nick returned from his weeks in Michigan with Mary. We had eaten, between the three of us, what seemed like three pounds of pasta. Nick had the largest amount, having employed his own unique method of packing it into his mouth in fistfuls. The sky was purple out the back window of the house. Some kind of early autumn sign, I thought, of what was coming next. And Nick had done the unthinkable: without being prodded, or even announcing his plans, he'd called the elevator to take him up to his bed, where he fell deeply asleep, his little pasta-laden belly rising and falling.

I watched as Paul covered his son and shut the creaking door. Paul directed me onto the porch out back, and we sat in his rain-rotten deck chairs. Above us, at the edge of the yard, the crows shifted from one power line to another.

"You want a beer?" Paul asked.

"Maybe later," I said. "I'm as full as I want to be."

"Good pasta." Paul looked out at the yard as if he were telling this to the crows. And then he jumped up, and announced, "Music." He disappeared inside. A low, crying harmonica warbled out of the room behind the sliding back doors. It sounded like Bob Dylan, but the song itself was unfamiliar. When Paul returned I pointed to the crows. They seemed to be listening, one of them nodding its beak.

"Will the music wake Nick?" I asked.

Paul shook his head. He knew what woke the boy. Paul had been taking care of him on his own long enough. He'd passed through the chaos of the early months, and the joy of the middle months, into the stark routine reality of this day and the next day and the day after that. Single parenthood made Paul feel like a man who'd been to war. But it was a good war. He'd been shocked, scarred, tired to the bones of his feet. But now he understood the very particular and strange doings of his son and loved almost all of them. Though things always seemed to be in a state of slow change, he would manage, at least until peer pressure turned everything in some new direction. The Spiderman years, thankfully, were still somewhere off in the distance.

"Are you," Paul wondered, "still free on Sunday?"

I was. I had agreed to take Nick for the day so Paul could get some shopping done. A rare opportunity to have Nick to myself.

"Good," he said, and dug into his pocket, down to the folds of his ratty deck chair. He came up with something silver, half hidden in his fist.

"I got this for you to give him." Paul passed the object over to me. It was a harmonica.

"E," Paul said.

"Sorry?"

"E. It's a weird key. But if he can get the hang of it he's on track. You be the harmonica giver. Tell him to push and pull."

I held the harmonica. It was cold in my hand, and without thinking I raised it to my nose. It smelled like well-worn pennies. The kind we used to put out on the railroad tracks and retrieve, once the train had flattened them into curled silver and copper pancakes.

"It smells old."

"It is. It was my dad's."

Ah, I thought. I might have seen it coming. All evening Paul had seemed pensive, or maybe just tired. But I should have guessed what it was he was mulling over.

"You know, my dad was a jazz fan. That was the only

music he cared about. Sometimes, when I was a kid, he took me to the clubs. After he'd been gone a while, I got up the guts to look through the records he left behind. We threw out so much of his stuff, but something made my mother save the records. They had been hers, I guess, just as much as they belonged to my father. There was nothing but jazz. But jazz of a very particular kind. The stuff recorded in New York, in recording studios on Broadway, and from time to time in New Jersey, from the mid-forties till the late fifties. Let's say, fifteen years' worth. The guys that recorded these records lived and played within a hundred or so blocks between Harlem and Greenwich Village. They were consummate individualists. They wanted no such thing as conventionality in their lives. Some wrecked themselves with drugs. Or wound up committed to psych wards, punched one too many times by the cops. The cops back then, I can tell you, were not considered to be local heroes. Some, like Monk—in fact my dad didn't care for Monk—ran out of steam or came to hate themselves and the world. They spent their final years silent.

"So I don't know what led him to buy tickets to Bob Dylan's 1964 concert at Philharmonic Hall. Maybe some girl he was seeing on the side. Or it's possible that for a week he allowed himself to be swept up in the buzz around the Village folk scene.

"Anyway, whatever the reason, he was there. I can't say whether he liked what Dylan was up to. And I don't think he'd have been taken in by the duets with Joan Baez. That would have been kid stuff to him. But something happened there all the same. Between songs, Dylan was fumbling around. Deciding what to play next. And he called out to the audience, Anyone got an E harmonica? Well, you know, it was New York in 1964. These were Dylan fans. Not just fans. Devotees. E harmonicas came raining down from the rafters. And that one," Paul pointed at the instrument nesting in my hands, "bounced off the head of the guy sitting in front of my dad and landed in his lap. Nutty, eh?"

The evening had grown cool and the crows had fluttered off to another perch. The music inside had stopped.

"Give it to the kid on Sunday," Paul said. "If you give it, instead of me, it won't be just one more thing from the old man."

❨On Sunday I knocked on Paul's door around ten. For a longish time there was no response. Then Nick, from behind the door, shouted, "Daddy. Dada. He's here!"

Paul opened the door and Nick came bursting out. He grabbed me around the legs. "Let's go," he shouted. "Let's play. At the park. Let's go now."

We waited while Paul got himself ready, and then watched as he hopped on his clattery old bike. He'd picked it up off a neighbour's front lawn, but only after knocking on the front door to ask if it had been left out for someone to take. Off he rode. Free for the rest of the morning and the afternoon. As he turned the corner, waving back at us, Nick's father reminded me of a child himself, setting out purposefully and with bravura, as if to prove he really would be fine on his own.

It was oddly quiet at Nick's neighbourhood park. A few parents meandered around behind their kids. The city hadn't bothered to clear last fall's leaves, so there was an odd mixture of smells—the warm lake air, the heated tarmac, but then add to that, in certain corners down near the ground where children like to play, the musk of rotten leaves. Nick had brought a bag of his trains and set about driving them in carefully organized groups along a low wooden wall that skirted the swings and slide. He pushed one of his favourites far out, away from where I sat, then worked the others over to that spot, giving him the opportunity to bring them all back to where he'd started.

There was something very slow and sweet and open-ended about Nick's little boy's business. It felt as though it could go on forever, that we wouldn't need a thing—not food, or companionship, nor comfort of home, nothing beyond the surrounding park with its scents and views. Night could come, then morning, and another day, and still we would keep ourselves busy, alone under the sky. For what seemed like an hour I pushed him on a swing. He became quiet, seemingly contemplative, as I counted sets of ten pushes. When I asked if he was okay, he whispered, "Watch the sky. It's beautiful, isn't it?"

Where did he hear that? I wondered. As if it mattered.

We stayed well past lunch, then made our way home. When dinnertime rolled around and Paul still hadn't appeared, I began to wonder if we hadn't missed a call while we were at the park. But then, why wouldn't he just call again?

I put Nick to bed and spent the night on Paul's couch, waking every few hours. I had to remind myself each time I awoke why I was in my friend's darkened living room and not at home in my own bed. Nick got out of bed at seven. When he discovered that his father was still not home, he began to cry.

He demanded ice cream for breakfast and I didn't hesitate to give him a full bowl. He sat at the kitchen table holding a spoon of the stuff near his mouth, carefully touching it with the tip of his tongue. Eating a bowl of ice cream this way could easily take a week.

I put the harmonica down beside him. He didn't notice it at first. Then he put his hand on it, raised it to his mouth, and began puffing on it, running it quickly from one side of his mouth to the other. The effect was immediate. He hopped down from his chair and marched off, knees high, exploring his new powers. He was out on the back deck with the crows when the phone rang. My heart sank just to hear it.

"Who are you?" the caller asked. Was there a next of kin there? Yes, I explained, but that kin was a child. The caller paused. Then she just gave it up: Paul had been crushed against a parked car by a city bus. Eyewitnesses disagreed on whose fault it was. But I was to be assured there would be a full investigation. This was the worst news imaginable. The whole picture had not yet come clear—I was numb, listening to the woman's voice on the line, while trying to keep Nick under wraps—when the phone went dead. Nick stood, holding the unplugged line in his hand, saying, "I want to say hi!"

The effect was almost funny. We plugged the phone back in and I ordered Nick out into the backyard. I followed and stood beside him. We agreed to wait for the next ring. But it didn't come. Nick placed himself at the deck's railing and blew whining blasts.

I felt I'd heard news of Paul in a dream. I could not say what the true point of the call had been. Was he alive or dead? If alive, to which hospital were we meant to go? Somehow, the caller had believed she'd completed her task. Or she had been distracted and simply forgotten us. Paul's calamity lay in a file on her desk, and she'd gone out for a smoke.

"Is this a note?" Nick asked, then drew a broad, rough sound out of the harmonica. It rang, Dylanesque and strange in the backyard.

Across the way Paul's neighbour heard the music and looked our way. He waved as he walked nimbly on wooden planks to pick the round red tomatoes from their vines. As he worked I thought I caught the scent of the plucked vines, the red weights piling in an old wicker basket. Nick watched too, looking proprietary, serious, calm. Then he went back to playing one note after another. Above us on the high wire the crows shuddered and took flight.

SEPTEMBER SONG

On Bloor Street, a trampy looking character was strumming a beat-up guitar. I recognized the song—something from the second side of *Blonde on Blonde*. The version was slow and out of tune, but still, the song shone through. As I listened, I thought of Nick, who loved the most surreal Dylan lyrics. We had traded them like a vaudeville team. "I'm taking my potatoes down to be mashed," he would shout, in response to my "What's it to you Moby Dick? This is Chicken town." The guitar tramp began a lengthy effort to tune his guitar, and who should turn the corner but Paul. I hadn't seen him in weeks. He was walking with a cane, and he'd grown out the Kerouac cut.

He said he was shattered, a shadow of himself. That he wasn't calling anyone. Nothing personal.

It was all right, I told him, though we both knew it wasn't all right. Not at all.

The worst part of everything that had happened, he said, was that after the accident he couldn't take care of Nick. Mary had come up from Michigan and taken him down to the prize winning garden and the firm handshake. It was only for the short run, but it felt like a bad dream. Like he hadn't been crushed, but killed. He said he felt the bus driver had done it on purpose—to show him who really was boss—and then the goddamn cop who came by to write things up was clearly on the driver's side of the story, not listening to anything but his bleating excuses about how Paul's bike had come out of nowhere.

It wasn't true, Paul said. The bus had cut him off, squeezed in too tight as he passed and flattened him up against the door of a parked car. Those bastards had stolen his kid from him. And this had loosened a whole raft of black thoughts in his head.

I asked him what these were.

He paused, deciding if he should tell me more. "I sold the Nash," he said. "After the accident I didn't want it anymore. A guy came to the door with an envelope full of hundred dollar bills and I just let it go. But since then I've been having this recurring dream. A new one altogether."

The street crowd rushed past. The brick buildings were peach-coloured in the low sun. And the fall air was cool and crisp with change. "In the dream I'm a kind of ghost. I find an old car with the key in the ignition. I get in, and all day and night I drive it around the city. Some people notice. But most don't. In the dream it's clear what I am to the ones who do see me. I'm their past going by."

I didn't know what to say about this. I never know what dreams mean. So I told him about that Sunday with Nick in the park. He nodded. It was the sort of thing I thought he would want to hear. We stood like that, to the accompaniment of coins dropping in the guitarist's paper cup.

It was fall. The boy was far away. We shook hands lightly. He went up the block and stood at the curb, waiting for the light to change. Then he turned the corner and was gone. My time with the boy and his father seemed to evaporate then, to rise with the noise and movement of the street and disappear into the low light of day.

Shelley Butler, Howard Dancyger, Steven Hayward, Susan Haley and Eric Siblin read and helped make this a better book. Andrew Steeves made it look great to hold in your hand. —NR

Gaspereau Press acknowledges the support of the Canada Council for the Arts and the Nova Scotia Department of Tourism, Culture & Heritage.

This is a work of fiction and not a literal depiction.

Typeset in Robert Slimbach's Adobe Jenson by Andrew Steeves and printed and bound under the direction of Gary Dunfield at Gaspereau Press.

1 3 5 7 6 4 2

Library & Archives Canada Cataloguing in Publication

Ravvin, Norman, 1963–
The joyful child / Norman Ravvin.

ISBN 978-1-55447-087-7
I. Title.

PS8585.A8735J69 2010 C813'.54 C2010-905870-4

GASPEREAU PRESS LIMITED ☾ GARY DUNFIELD
& ANDREW STEEVES ☾ PRINTERS & PUBLISHERS
47 Church Avenue, Kentville, Nova Scotia, Canada B4N 2M7